ART OF THE WORLD

NON-EUROPEAN CULTURES

THE HISTORICAL, SOCIOLOGICAL

AND RELIGIOUS BACKGROUNDS

THE ART OF
CHINESE LANDSCAPE PAINTING

IN THE CAVES OF TUN-HUANG

ANIL DE SILVA

PHOTOGRAPHS BY DOMINIQUE DARBOIS

CROWN PUBLISHERS, INC., NEW YORK

Title-page: Fresco from Cave 323 at Tun-huang: detail. T'ang dynasty. The pagoda depicted resembles one of the earliest wooden pagodas at Hokiji near Nara, Japan, which is square in plan and is built in the Chinese T'ang style. *Cf. p. 146.*

All photographs of the Tun-huang Caves in this volume have been taken with the kind permission of the Tun-huang Institute. Many of them are reproduced here for the first time in color.

FIRST PUBLISHED IN 1964

GERMAN EDITION 1964 © HOLLE VERLAG G.M.B.H., BADEN-BADEN, GERMANY

ENGLISH TRANSLATION © 1967 BY HOLLE VERLAG, G.M.B.H., BADEN-BADEN, GERMANY

LIBRARY OF CONGRESS CATALOG CARD NUMBER: 67-19591

PRINTED IN HOLLAND

CONTENTS

List of colour plates (6). List of monochrome plates (6). List of figures (7).
Acknowledgments (7).

FOREWORD 9

INTRODUCTION 15

  I. PRE-HAN ART 33

  II. THE HAN DYNASTY (206 B.C.–A.D. 220) 53

  III. THE THREE KINGDOMS AND THE SIX DYNASTIES
     (A.D. 220–589) 75

  IV. THE SUI DYNASTY (A.D. 589–618) 105

  V. THE T'ANG DYNASTY (A.D. 618–906) 133

  VI. THE SUNG DYNASTY (A.D. 960–1279) 181

CONCLUSIONS 202

APPENDIX 213

Map: Central Asia and the Silk Road (214–5). Chronological table (216).
List of caves (224). Bibliography (225). Index (229).

LIST OF COLOUR PLATES

Cave 323	3	Cave 323	144, 145
Cave complex of Tun-huang	21	Cave 209	149
Shell with hunting scene	46	Cave 217	155, 157
Polychrome painted funerary tile	49	Cave 45	158
Painted clay brick	64	Cave 205	166, 169
Cave 257	77, 79, 81	Cave 320	167
Cave 428	82, 85	Cave 172	171
Cave 285	98, 99	Cave 198	175
Cave 296	108, 110	Cave 112	176, 177
Cave 302	117, 118–9	Cave 196	178, 179
Cave 299	120–1	Cave 186	186
Cave 303	126	Cave 288	190
Cave 423	128–9	Cave 332	193
Apsara strewing flowers	132	Cave 61	195, 197
Cave 103	137	Cave 55	198
Cave 321	139		

LIST OF MONOCHROME PLATES

City gate at Tun-huang	17 above	Cave 296	111
Ox-cart	17 below	Cave 302	112
River-bed at Tun-huang	18 above	Cave 301	113
Sand cliff	18 below	Cave 420	114 above
Caves at Tun-huang: detail	27	Cave 419	114 below
Caves at Tun-huang: detail	28	Cave 419	123 above
Clay brick: detail	37	Cave 420	123 below
Assyrian hunting relief	38	Cave 419	124
Apsara	51	Country house of the poet Wang Wei:	
Clay panel from tomb	52	painting	141
Bronze vase, so-called 'hunting bronze'	57	Cave 103	142
Frescoes in a tomb: details	58–59	Cave 323	151
Detail of bronze vase on p. 57	60	Cave 209	152
Scroll: detail	73	Cave 217	161
Cave 285	74	Cave 45	162–3, 164
Cave 249	87, 88	Cave 369	173
Cave 428	93 above	Cave 112	174
Panel in relief	93 below	Cave 321	183
Cave 285	94–95	Horizontal scroll: detail	184
Cave 428	96	Cave 61	205
Cave 299	101	Cave 55	206, 207
Tripod with lid	102	Rubbing from stamped brick	208

LIST OF FIGURES

1 – Motifs: water, river, wood (or tree), forest 40
2 – Stone rubbing 41
3 – Funerary urn 41
4 – Rubbing from stone relief 42
5 – Bronze with inlays 43
6 – Rubbing from stone relief 43
7 – Rubbing from stone relief 44–45
8 – Detail of bronze tube 47
9–12 – Various types of tree 48
13 – Bronze basin 48
14 – Stamped brick 55
15 – Stamped brick from tomb 62
16 – Stamped brick 63
17 – Rubbing from stone panel 65
18 – Rubbing from stone panel 66
19 – Rubbing from stone panel 68–69
20 – Rubbing from stone panel 68
21 – Rubbing from brick 69
22 – Neolithic pot 70
23 – Rubbing from engraved bone 71
24 – Spirit riding on clouds 86
25 – Dragon: stone relief 90
26 – Painting ascribed to Tung Yüan 91
27 – Painting ascribed to Hsü Tao-ning 103
28 – Painting ascribed to Kuo Hsi 103
29 – Rubbing from stone relief 104
30 – Lacquer 106
31 – Rubbing from stone sarcophagus 109
32–A–L – Various types of tree 130–1
33 – Rubbing from Han relief 160

ACKNOWLEDGMENTS

The following museums and institutions kindly allowed reproduction of the plates on the following pages:

Cleveland Museum of Art 46
Musée Guimet, Paris 51
Museum of Fine Arts, Boston 49, 64, 184
Pillsbury Collection, Minneapolis Museum 57
Minneapolis Institute of Arts 102
Stiftung Preussischer Kulturbesitz, Indische Kunstabteilung, Berlin 132
British Museum, London 141

The map on p. 214–5 was drawn by Heinz Prüstel of Mainz, who also executed the figures from data supplied by the author.

FOREWORD

I understand painting by my natural disposition as
well as the crying crane knows his way through the
night . . . my love of landscapes has led me on.

If I presume to begin with the words of Wang Wei, it is because
'the love of landscapes has led me on' to undertake this study; this
may in some fashion excuse the shortcomings of this book.

To me as a Buddhist there is more in the study of landscape painting
than the wish to share my enthusiasm; there is the desire to search
for the meaning behind the pictures; as Dr Sirén says, 'the search
is the gist of the matter; it increases the experience, warms the
heart, opens the eyes . . .' – this then is my justification.

I went to Tun-huang with Dominique Darbois, the photographer,
and Romila Thapar of London University after we had completed a
photographic documentation of the Western Caves of Mai-chi Shan
in Kansu province. We had worked there for several weeks and
taken over seven hundred photographs, several hundred of them
in colour. But the experience gained in this work did not really
help me in the choice of the photographs to be taken in Tun-huang.
When we arrived, we were confronted with four hundred and
sixty-nine caves to be inspected before I could actually decide which
scenes we could photograph. The time and the number of photographs we could take were limited, and the task of choosing seventy
landscapes from the incredible wealth that lay before us was extremely difficult; even though I was in some measure prepared,
the richness of colour and line was intoxicating. It took nearly a
week to go through the caves, stopping only long enough to examine
each one briefly. In the meantime the work of photography had
to begin, for the complicated task of taking pictures both in black
and white and in colour can be understood only by someone who
has attempted it. Decisions had to be taken quickly, and indeed if

I had the opportunity again my choice might be slightly different. I would like to draw attention to two points. The first is the matter of dating and numbering the caves. In both cases I have followed the dates and numbers as given by the Tun-huang Institute.

The second is the question of the identification of the plates themselves. Chinese Buddhist iconography is often a complex and baffling subject; Dr Waley has drawn attention to the fact that at Tun-huang some of the pictures may illustrate popular *p'ien-wên* or 'wonder writings' whereas others are probably based on uncanonical folklore. He also emphasizes the fact that paintings were sometimes based on dreams or visions and not on a text. This of course makes a difficult subject even more difficult.

Since this volume was completed in 1959 other contributions to the subject have appeared which have analysed in detail a wealth of material, including some of the early Tun-huang landscape paintings that are treated here. Frequently there is misunderstanding about the total effect of these frescoes.

Only those who have actually seen the caves can really visualize the general impression evoked by these pictures. Yet this general impression is the most important achievement of the Tun-huang artists. In some of the caves they showed genius in the way in which they divided and arranged the wall surfaces; there is an almost perfect rhythm in the juxtaposition of the various elements. Undoubtedly there are occasional instances of 'archaism', but does this diminish the artistic value of a painting? An artist loses none of his greatness if his work is more primitive than those produced by others; just as little does a developed technique – for example, in rendering space in depth or perspective – imply greater aesthetic value. It is always dangerous, one might say, to take the achievements of a particular period of artistic development as the yardstick in evaluating works produced earlier. Do we appreciate Romanesque art less than that of the Renaissance or of later periods simply because it has some archaic features?

PLATES PP. 77, 79, 81, 94, 95, 98, 99 Two early caves – 257 and 285 – which are dealt with in this book contain some of the finest frescoes known to me. In Cave 285 the use of delicate lines produces a total effect of abundant vitality and enchanting beauty. In Cave 257 the strong colours convey an intensity of feeling and a serene dignity that are reminiscent of Piero della Francesca.

To evaluate properly the treatment of line and the brushwork the prime necessity is to have good photographs, such as have been used to illustrate this volume. Unfortunately some of our colour plates have had to be greatly reduced in size, and this naturally makes it more difficult to appreciate them.

In many caves, such as 296, 299, 249 and 302, the artists made no attempt to solve the problem of representing space in depth. These paintings are distinguished by serene and flowing lines, so that the general effect is one of unforgettable charm. It is the quality of the draughtsmanhip that is of importance: it shows such spontaneity and dedication that one experiences complete satisfaction.

PLATES PP. 87–88, 108, 111, 117, 118–9, 120–1

We certainly do not seek to belittle the studies that have been made hitherto when we state that a reproduction on a reduced scale is no substitute for the experience derived from looking at the original. But the present volume is based upon such an experience. The author has had the good fortune to be able to compare the colours and aesthetic effect of reproductions with those of the actual wall-paintings at Tun-huang. This, in our estimation, gives the work such value and significance as it possesses. It is written in the hope that it may contribute in some measure towards a better understanding of these masterpieces.

Most of these plates are published in colour for the first time in Europe; a few of them appeared in the Christmas 1958 issue of *Plaisirs de France*.

There are two categories of people to whom I am deeply indebted; those who were responsible for making this trip possible and who helped us while we were there, and those who have aided me while actually writing the book itself.

Among the former I am indebted to His Excellency the late Sardar K. Panikkar and Her Excellency Madame Rajan Nehru, Indian Ambassadress in Peking; the first for helping this project through, and the second for her sympathy and assistance while we were in China at all moments of stress and strain; to Dr Hsia Nai, Director of the Department of Archaeology, Academia Sinica, Peking, who gave me all possible co-operation, even after my return; to Dr Chang Shu-hung, Director of the Tun-huang Research Institute, for his hospitality, kindness and invariable helpfulness in all our daily work, and for showing us an example of devotion to Ch'ien-fo Tung (i.e. Caves of a Thousand Buddhas) that is a source of inspiration to all who were fortunate enough to visit the Institute; to my interpreter Myngoo Wong, who helped me to translate Chinese texts in addition to her daily work as interpreter. Dominique Darbois worked unsparingly and I would like to thank her here for her total disregard of fatigue and in some instances, as in Mai-chi Shan, even of danger.

This study does not claim to be completely new or entirely without error. It is of necessity based on the work of others, particularly the two sinologists of very great stature, Dr Osvald Sirén and Dr Arthur Waley, to whose writings and translations every non-Chinese owes a great deal. I must thank Dr Waley for sparing me the time to go over the plates and for making valuable suggestions about them. I would also like to remember my former professor, the late Jean Buhot, who was always generous and understanding. If he were alive, I am sure his help and guidance would have added infinitely to this study, and I have felt his loss continually.

But there are so many persons who have been helpful and kind that I can only think of an old saying, 'when the heart is deeply grateful, there are no words to express it.' This is particularly true of Dr Chêng Tê-k'un, Lecturer in Chinese Archaeology at Cambridge University, and Dr Joseph Needham, author of *Chinese Art*. Dr Chêng Tê-k'un not only read through my whole manuscript, but continually supplied me with valuable indications and translated some of the inscriptions on the tablets in the plates. Dr Needham let me read certain extracts from his then still unpublished fourth volume of *Science and Civilization in China*, and gave me other pertinent material. All three have aided me most generously. John Lust, assistant librarian of the School of Oriental and African

Studies, was invariably helpful in getting me the necessary books. Paul Braisted, President of the Hazen Foundation, sent me the photographs from the American museums used in the illustrations. In concluding I should like to say how deeply thankful I am for the opportunity given me to visit Tun-huang. Ever since my earliest years, when I read the memoirs of Hsüan Tsang and adopted him as a sort of patron saint, his extraordinary journey through the Gobi to India in search of truth stimulated and inspired me.

Anil de Silva

INTRODUCTION

Year by year if it is not the Golden River
it is the Jade Gate Pass.
Morning after morning we take up whips
and gird on our swords.
Through the white snow of three springs
we have buried our comrades in green tombs of exile.
Where for ten thousand *li* the Yellow River
winds its way through the Black Hills.[1]

Lu Chu Yung
(9th century A.D.)

The Silk Road, the oldest trade-route known to man, used in pre-historic times for the exchange of bronze and furs, stretched from the shores of the Mediterranean to the Great Wall. It was firmly established by the first century B.C., and it was the route along which jade found its way from China to the West and which enabled caravans laden with lacquer and silk to reach all parts of the then known world.

Semi-diplomatic and commercial missions starting from the eastern provinces of the Roman Empire, the Middle East, Bactria, Samarkand and India crossed the Central Asian region, reaching the silk markets of the Tarim basin by two desert routes which met at the frontier town of Tun-huang. This territory was encompassed by immense mountains – the massifs of Karakorum and K'un-lun in the south and the Celestial Mountains (T'ien Shan) in the north. The southern road, coming from India, passed through Yarkand, Khotan and Mirān, the northern route by way of the Pamirs and the oasis of Kashgar, Kuchā, Kyzyl and Turfan. They were the principal arteries for trade and the transmission of religious and scientific ideas. These Central Asian kingdoms along the Silk Road were rich flourishing gardens in the desert. Such famous travellers

---

[1] Based upon a translation by E. Chavannes.

as Hsüan Tsang in the seventh and Marco Polo in the thirteenth century have left us vivid descriptions of their beauty. The hardships of the journey over snow-clad passes and across burning sands were relieved only by the luxury and plenty found in these romantic oasis cities.

The frescoes from the cave-temples in these kingdoms show splendid horsemen, presumably just like those whom Hsüan Tsang describes as riding out to meet him when he arrived on his way to India. These cavaliers wore high boots and riding-coats of silk falling to the knees and taken in at the waist with metal belts. Their tunics of blue, grey, white and olive green were embroidered with pearls and lined and trimmed with fur. They must have presented a splendid sight with their coloured and gilded banners and their standards sculptured and painted with heraldic animals such as the tiger or the dragon.

Marco Polo seems to have taken the southern route for, speaking of Khotan, he says, 'everything necessary for human life is here in the greatest plenty – cotton, flax, hemp, grain, wine. The inhabitants cultivate farms and vineyards and have numerous gardens. They also make a living by trade and manufacture.'

But moments of relaxation in these desert cities, with their refinement and luxury, did not overcome the fear of the desert that filled the hearts of even such intrepid merchants as the Chinese. As late as the thirteenth century Marco Polo says, 'it is a well-established opinion that the desert is inhabited by spirits who call the travellers by their names and speak to them as if they were their companions, thus leading them into the abyss. One hears the sound of music; of arms and tambours . . .'

With these merchant caravans – laden with Alexandrian glassware (particularly welcome all over Asia), silk, spices, ivory and elephants from India for the Roman armies, precious stones, jade, coral,

Page 17 above: Ming Gate, one of the entrances to the walled oasis town of Tun-huang. *Cf. p. 24*
Page 17 below: The two-wheeled ox-cart is still widely used today; its form has not changed for many centuries and identical ones are to be found on the Tun-huang frescoes. *Cf. Plate on p. 126*

amber and crystal – came widely differing types of people. Syrian jugglers and acrobats mingled with diplomats and high priests. Christians, Hindus and Buddhists lived side by side, and at Tun-huang, as in all the other Central Asian kingdoms, a hybrid population came into being.

Though this route was used even by Byzantine envoys, in the thirteenth century the Silk Road became far safer for travel as a result of the Mongol consolidation of power in this region. Astonishingly accurate accounts have been left both by Western and by Chinese travellers describing such battles as the crossing of the Yangtze by the Sui and the sieges of the Byzantines by the Arabs, both in the seventh century. These memoirs disclose a picture of the great exchange of technical, scientific and religious ideas that took place between East and West. Guillaume Bouchier, for example, a Parisian goldsmith, worked in this region in the thirteenth century and was surely responsible for the fleur-de-lys motif painted on the robes of Buddha images (Needham). Kumārajīva, son of an Indian father and Princess Jīva of Kuchā, became the most renowned Buddhist teacher in China. The Han emperor Wu Ti, in the second century B.C., extended the Great Wall both as a protection against the Hun invaders and as a barrier preventing the inhabitants from mixing with 'foreign barbarians'. Never has a fortification had such terrible associations for the people it was designed to protect. 'The bones of millions of men are buried in the Great Wall,' runs an old saying, and this is the theme of many Chinese folk-songs.

As in most periods of expansion, the splendour of the Han Empire (206 B.C.–A.D. 220) was built on much human misery. Later poets, in particular the great Li Po, sang of the desolate cries of the lost men who built the Wall:

Page 18 above: Only a few kilometres from the oasis of Tun-huang is a quiet valley, its river in summer no more than a stream. *Cf. p. 24*

Page 18 below: A sand cliff rises vertically from the desert plain. On the left one can see the Caves of the Thousand Buddhas, cut directly into the cliff-face; on the right, in the desert, one can make out the bright stūpas raised over the monks' burial-places. *Cf. p. 24*

Better for a man to die fighting;
How can one support the sorrow of oppression
While building the Great Wall?
The Great Wall it goes without end,
It runs three thousand *li* over the earth.[2]

The builders perished at their task. 'Alas, the dry bones on the shores of the Wu-Ting are still men who appear in the dreams of their loved ones.'

To consolidate the Great Wall, the Han emperors constructed an uninterrupted line of forts which ran from Chiu-ch'üan (the Fountain of Wine) to the east, passed north of Tun-huang, and across the salt marshes to the west. These fortifications were similar to those built by the Romans. History proved the utility of this construction, for throughout the centuries Tun-huang and the other forts were constantly subjected to attack. An anonymous poet wrote:

Bitter sorrow it is to inhabit the frontier.
Three of my sons went to Tun-huang,
Another sent to Lung-hai,
The fifth still further West,
Their five wives are pregnant.[3]

The entire region was made an administrative area in 105 B.C. after General Ho Ch'ü-ping's brilliant victory over the Huns in 121 B.C. The foundation of Tun-huang dates back to this epoch, and the following imperial edict to the governor of the nearby fortress of Chiu-ch'üan explains its origin.

'Two thousand soldiers together with generals and officials are to proceed to occupy a locality in order to establish there an agricultural colony. It will be the duty of the governor to examine the configuration of this place and by utilizing natural obstacles a rampart will be constructed in order to exercise control. Let there be no negligence of any kind, and let the orders be conformed to.'[4]

[2] Based upon a translation by E. Chavannes.
[3] Based upon a translation by E. Chavannes.
[4] Based upon a translation by E. Chavannes.

A wall of the cave complex at Tun-huang. One can clearly see how the caves are cut into the cliff-face. On the walls of the caves one can make out paintings that have faded as a result of weathering. *Cf. p. 24*

The governor of Tun-huang was the chief administrator of the western fortification, which was divided into several sectors under different military commanders. The 'Yü-Mên', or the Jade Gate, was one of these sectors, and soldiers from distant provinces, Shansi, Szechwan, Honan and Kiangsu were sent here for border service. Many of the men were deported convicts.

Watch-towers were distributed over the entire region; they were equipped with fire signals to warn of the approach of an enemy, as were those constructed by the Genoese much later along the shores of the Mediterranean.

In the nineteenth and early twentieth centuries European explorers and travellers, Kropotkin the Russian, Sven Hedin the Swede, Bonin the Frenchman, and Sir Aurel Stein the Englishman discovered traces of these Han garrisons and watch-towers. Nothing is more poignant and revealing of this past and its human drama than the objects brought to light after two thousand years. The Han rubbish-dumps buried near the walls contained horse dung and dried branches of poplar for fires, an inscribed box containing one hundred bronze arrow-heads belonging to the Chu-chüeh company; pottery, spoons, combs, woven string shoes, beating rods, dice and silk rolls, documents on wood, paper, leather and silk; dated records of A.D. 17; folded and addressed letters, calendars, writing-slips and books (Stein).

We learn from these documents that capital punishment was carried out only after an application to the Throne, but corporal punishment (as in most armies until the nineteenth century) could be administered up to two hundred and thirty strokes. The men, simple soldiers torn from their loved ones, dreaded the icy wind which 'goes whistling through the Gate of Jade.' Yet the writing-slips on which they strove to improve their calligraphy are a silent witness to their efforts to better themselves in spite of such terrible conditions.

Even so far from the heart of the empire, the remains of quantities of books have been found, including a large number of primers and such classics as Liu Hsiang's *Biographies of Eminent Women*, written at the end of the first century A.D. (Stein).

The strategic importance of Tun-huang is evident from the story that in *circa* 104 B.C. the Son of Heaven fell into a violent rage when he heard the news that General Li Kuang-li, who had ridden out of the city with ten thousand men to meet the Ta-Wan (Ferghana), had been defeated. The emperor immediately sent emissaries to close the Jade Gate and declared that any member of the defeated army who ventured to enter the city would at once be decapitated. General Li Kuang-li 'was overcome with fear and remained at Tun-huang,' we are told. The emperor, however, later relented, as he sent the general for his second and victorious expedition some sixty thousand men, not counting camp-followers, thirty thousand horses, and one hundred thousand cattle (Stein). The deployment of such forces would strain the resources of any city, even today.

Beyond the western limits of the Great Wall and its Jade Gate, in the vast desert valley of the Su-lo Ho, lie the green oasis of Tun-huang and Ch'ien-fo Tung, the Caves of a Thousand Buddhas. One thousand miles from Peking, watered by the perpetual snows on the Nan Shan ranges, it was the base from which China advanced across the Great Gobi into the Tarim basin and the Celestial Mountains.

When one reaches the airport of Chiu-ch'üan, one sees ranges of bare weathered hills and in the background the deep blue of the snow-capped Nan Shan. The rest of the journey is by jeep, which takes the new desert road, while the horse-drawn carts with their curiously large wheels (the same as those painted in the frescoes of the caves) follow the old track taken by explorers and archaeologists such as Aurel Stein and Paul Pelliot. PLATE P. 17 BELOW

Tall poplars seem to emerge from the blue waters of a lake shimmering in the heat, with curious rocks reflected in its milky surface; this vision is like some long-forgotten mirror, reflecting a dream; it is a mirage, receding before us as we advance, and it is this vision that is so often painted on the walls of the Caves of Ch'ien-fo Tung. A herd of gazelles scatters towards the hills. The wheels of the carts creak piercingly as they wend their way; hundreds of lorries pound

23

along what may now be called the oil road, for upon the arid slopes and hills the black derricks of the oil-fields stand out against purplish red, yellow and pink peaks.

Passing the oasis town of Tun-huang after eleven hours on the road, we turn left and drive fifteen kilometres further into the desert; we enter a silent valley, the wide river-bed in summer holding only a stream. Suddenly the greenish-grey spurs of a sand ridge rise perpendicularly out of the desert from north to south. Here, dug directly into the sand cliff, are the first caves. 'A multitude of dark cavities honeycomb the sombre rock in irregular tiers. From the foot of the precipice flights of steps connect the grottoes, the whole resembling the troglodyte dwellings of anchorites seen in early Italian paintings.'[5]

The bells of the Ming gateway ring out softly as we drive under the rustling branches, the hour is sunset, and the outline of distant mountains, the white plastered wall, the tops of the trees, the vast desert beyond the river-bed, the luminous stūpas where the monks lie buried, the distant hills – all are incarnadine, glowing in a liquid crimson light.

From their foundation in A.D. 366 by the monk Lo Tsun the caves suffered repeatedly from invasions. The most important was in 763, when Tun-huang was conquered by the Tibetans. The monks were influential in bringing about the return of the region to imperial control on June 23, 848. In recognition of this the elders Hung Jên and Wu Chan were given ecclesiastical titles by the Son of Heaven; this rather wonderful letter was found among the documents walled up in one of the caves.

'O Master Hung Jên, you are an excellent child of China and a model of discipline for the western countries. Your conduct is pure and you guard in your most profound being the sword of intelligence. You continue, at a great distance, to cherish your ancient country. I confer on you the title of assistant to the altar beyond the capital, and I bestow on you the violet garment, so that you may be

PLATE P. 18
ABOVE

PLATE P. 18
BELOW

PLATES PP. 27, 28

PLATE P. 21

PLATE P. 17
ABOVE

---

[5] Sir Marc Aurel Stein, *Ruins of Desert Cathay*, London, 1912, vol. 2, p. 23.

resplendent among the sombre costumes of the barbarians. I do not know, O Master, if you will well support the heat of the summer . . . You have changed the hearts of these men of strange race, their irascible and violent spirit has been (through the sovereign doctrine) entirely suppressed.'[6]

The splendour of the monasteries has long since disappeared. At PLATE P. 27 one time there were over a thousand grottoes, and today there remain four hundred and sixty-nine chapels, their walls magnificently covered with frescoes. The rock is friable and unsuitable for carving. Before being painted, the walls were prepared with a first coat of mud mixed with dung, straw and animal hair and were finished off with a layer of white kaolin, used for making pottery. The colours employed in the paintings were malachite green, azurite blue, orpiment yellow, iron oxide or earth red, vermilion or cinnabar, gold-leaf, lamp black, white lead, kaolin and red lead; the pigments were mixed with glue and painted on to the prepared wall surface. The technique was not usually al fresco, although they are generally referred to as frescoes. Many techniques seem to have been employed for the actual design, including free-hand drawings, stencils and compasses for the nimbuses or haloes. But whatever technique was used, the overall effect of the intricate and well-balanced compositions which cover the wall surface is one of incredible richness.

Chinese archaeologists have discovered that in a great many of the caves the walls have three different layers of frescoes, superimposed one upon the other. They correspond to frescoes painted at different epochs – for example, Wei, Sui and T'ang. The work involved in taking off each layer of paint without destroying the others and placing each layer in another location, poses a technical problem of the greatest magnitude. It could perhaps be undertaken by real international co-operation.

The survival of these caves is something of a miracle. One trembles at the thought that they were for over fifteen hundred years subject to barbarian invasions, and also exposed to erosion by the devastating

[6] Based upon a translation by E. Chavannes.

desert winds that sweep down from the north, 'the wind which sings in the trees of the Bodhi.'

In ancient times numerous monasteries lay among the groves of elms and poplars running alongside the caves. Today the plastered white buildings of the newly-constructed Tun-huang Research Institute lie under their swaying branches.

At the beginning of this century nearly twenty thousand MSS were discovered where they had been walled up in the eleventh century for protection against invaders. Having been forgotten for eight hundred years, they were found by Chinese workmen while repairing the wall of one of the larger caves. A great part of these texts, which are found in Europe, brought by Paul Pelliot and Sir Aurel Stein, are written in Chinese, Tibetan, Turki, Uighur, Tokharian, Brahmi and Old Persian. They were to cast a brilliant if fitful light on the extraordinary community of peoples that lived in Central Asia, and they have had a revolutionary effect on the study of Chinese literature, for they contain MSS of popular Buddhist narrative. This speaks for the importance of Tun-huang, for even today twenty thousand MSS would be considered a library of significance.

Paul Pelliot says that he felt intoxicated when the monk in charge opened the doors of the storehouse and he remembered the superstitious awe with which Petrarch looked upon Greek texts for the first time.

From the middle of the fourth century Tun-huang grew in importance as a centre, not only of trade, but of Buddhist learning, and is today the glorious repository of an unbroken tradition of Chinese painting from its foundation right up to the debased art of the Ch'ing dynasty in the nineteenth century. One thousand five hundred years of painting – one of the richest museums in the world. Tun-huang owes its greatness as a cultural centre to its benefactors: merchants, army commanders, religious societies, royal and princely donors.

Page 27: The caves, in irregular rows, are hewn into the rock, which is friable and unsuitable for carving.

Inscriptions on the walls bring us close to the men and women who donated them, for frequently these caves were for generations maintained by the same family or religious association. Cave 309, for example, was built by 'the Celestial Princess who bears the Li family name and who is the third daughter of the Great King-Emperor, by celestial brevet of the Great Kingdom of Yu t'ien (Khotan), (and who) makes this offering because she has recently become the wife of the Great Preceptor Ts'ao Yen (governor of Tun-huang).'[7]

Above another painting we read, 'the chief of the battalion of infantry Te Hang-chia, pure and pious, has reverently painted a representation of the Bodhisattva Kuan-shih-yin, in the hope that the souls of his father and mother will be born in the pure earth (Sukhāvatī) and that all members of his family, great and small, will find perpetual happiness. I make a vow that I, donor with a full heart, will present offerings and never cease to burn incense and will keep the lamps alight; this will serve to remind me in later years. In the fourth year of K'ai-pao, the sixth day of the ninth month (15th Oct. 972).'

A battalion commander of infantry at Tun-huang made an invocation 'with a full heart to Kuan-yin for her to protect the fortified towns so that the district will prosper and that the routes to the east towards China and to the west will be open and free; that in the north the Tartars and in the south the Tibetans cease their depredations and revolts. Third day of the seventh month of the fourth year of K'ai-yun (2nd Aug. 947).'[8]

As one enters a cave at Tun-huang and looks silently at the walls, the majestic calm of the Buddhas and other divinities, hieratically still and immense, contrast with the secular scenes where the life

[7] Based upon a translation by E. Chavannes.
[8] Based upon a translation by P. Pelliot.

Page 28: Steep steps lead up to the caves, which resemble the dwellings of troglodyte recluses that one encounters in early Italian paintings. Cf. p. 24

of man, the mere earth-dweller, continues on its mundane course. Busily he rushes around, be he prince or peasant, slave, soldier or merchant. Galloping cavaliers fight endless battles; merchants sail ships on rough seas; cavaliers venture forth from strong fortified cities for remote regions; pious devotees stand or kneel in reverence. Man ploughs, hunts, intrigues; dancing girls whirl to the music of ancient instruments in painted and sculptured pavilions, while the spiritual world of compassionate benevolence, the world of the eternal Buddhas, looks down upon it all.

In this world of man – the landscape of the Chinese countryside, the strange rocks, the waterfalls, the endless miles of fantastic mountains and plateaux, the trees, the lotus ponds, the wild mountain gorges – they continue their evolution from the early vigorous landscapes of the fifth century to the monochrome world of the eleventh-century Sung poets.

As can be imagined, the mingling of many races is reflected in the paintings. At Tun-huang a powerful Chinese idiom meets an equally strong tradition from India and Central Asia. This inevitably leads to an art that has its own individuality. But the spirit that dominates almost all the paintings, except those actually executed by foreigners, is Chinese. The old abstract swirling movement seen in cloud-scrolls and early bronzes is here and carries all before it. Never has this telling brush-stroke been produced by any other people except the Chinese. In some caves of the Wei, Sui and T'ang periods the movement is almost overwhelming. One can well understand that Wu Tao-tzǔ's painting was said to be 'so lively that the silk could hardly contain it.'

Tun-huang is not, as is often claimed, an isolated phenomenon, but can be closely integrated with all phases of Chinese painting. An inscription in Cave 321 informs us that an atelier for craftsmen was set up by the administration of the 'Sand and Melon county', as the region of Tun-huang was called.

The whole evolution of landscape painting as found in the frescoes of Tun-huang is closely linked with the most ancient tradition of Chinese art, as well as with the development of painting at court. As few Buddhist murals survive in other parts of the country, we know only from literature that the subjects treated here are similar to those painted by the great artists Ku K'ai-chih, Chang Sêng-yu, Wang Wei, Wu Tao-tzǔ, etc. It was from Tun-huang that Chinese landscape painting influenced the painting of Iran and Tibet, Central Asia and India. This influence also reached Indonesia and India by sea.

The three main forms of Chinese mountains spread over half the world. We find the stratified mountains as first seen in pre-Han bronzes, the cone-shaped variety, and mountains with trees along the ridges. They are seen in Sassanian silverware, Persian miniatures, Indian Jain MSS, and Javanese reliefs. Animal and human figures threading in and out of winding valleys are seen in Central Asia and Tibet.[9]

If Tun-huang disseminated Chinese techniques and ideas to the West, it was also the centre whence Western and Indian influence infiltrated into China; the use of shading to give the effect of volume (which probably came from India) seems to have started in Tun-huang earlier than in the rest of China.

Nowhere can the development of landscape painting be studied with such profit, and nowhere does it appear with such continuity as at Tun-huang.

[9] J. Auboyer, 'L'influence chinoise sur le paysage dans la peinture de l'Orient et dans le sculpture de l'Insulinde', in: *Revue des arts asiatiques*, Paris, 1935, vol. 9, no. 4, pp. 228 f.

I. PRE-HAN ART

There are landscapes in which one can travel, landscapes in which one may gaze, landscapes in which
one may ramble, and landscapes in which one may
dwell; any painting which reveals one of these is in
the category of the excellent.[1]

Kuo Hsi
(11th century A.D.)

China is one of the few countries in which there is an uninterrupted
development of art from the Neolithic past. It may even be unique
in this respect.

This study deals with the development of landscape painting in the
frescoes of Tun-huang between the fourth and eleventh centuries
A.D. To understand Chinese landscape painting, however, it is
essential to grasp first of all how the Chinese – and indeed the
Asian – approach to painting differs from that of Europe since the
Renaissance.

The basic elements in Chinese landscape painting can be followed
from the time of the Han dynasty (206 B.C.–A.D. 220), a period
which marked the turning-point of Chinese art and which saw a
solid foundation laid for a mode of expression whose development
has yet to be equalled in the history of painting. In the Han dynasty
the nameless monsters and bestial forms of Shang-Yin bronzes were
relegated to the past – to an age of antiquity – and men freed their
minds of their more fearful superstitions. Painters and poets breathed
a new air. They observed life and expressed it with a new freedom,
for 'the sun rose in the east and lit up the high dwellings' (Waley).
It is of this era that the eminent sinologist Professor Osvald Sirén
remarks that in all Chinese history no other period so combined
refinement with simplicity or displayed so well with simple line

[1] A. Waley, *An Introduction to the Study of Chinese Painting*, London, 1923, p. 190.

the beauty and character of objects. Yet as man grew out of his primitive state and entered an artificial environment of his own making, his intellectual consciousness developed and he became progressively more aware of his alienation from nature. It was this very sense of isolation that created the need for an intellectual and spiritual identification, or re-identification, with the natural things around him. The urge to identify himself with the whole of nature was a very strong one; man tried to recapture, by his intellect and spirit, in a conscious way, what he had lost by their growth. This search may lead to a very intense love of the terrestrial world. In the concept that all nature, whether living or inanimate, is a manifestation of the divine spirit, and in the belief that life may be reincarnated in different forms, the Oriental finds an intimate fraternity with the whole universe.

Three centuries before our era Taoist thought expressed this feeling; and there is a close affinity between the stories of the Taoist immortals and the conception of landscape painting. A legend concerning one of the *hsien* – as the Taoist mountain hermits are styled – bears directly on this point. He was said to possess the extraordinary power of contracting the veins of the earth so that a stretch of a thousand *li* came within the limits of vision. It would seem that the concept of landscape painting embodied in the maxim 'a thousand *li* to a single inch' is derived directly from this legend.

In this manner a number of typical features are condensed within a small compass in one painting to give the impression of a vast and seemingly endless landscape. The hundred *li* of a river or of a mountain range are presented as a whole, yet on closer scrutiny each detail of their multitudinous parts has its separate identity; but within and as part of the whole picture. Each detail, like man himself, is at the same time a separate entity and integrated with the natural world in which he lives.

To the European eye, used to pictorial representation from a single viewpoint, a fresco in the Ajantā cave-temples in India, for example, may at first appear as a haphazard composition with no spatial organization (Auboyer). Only gradually does one realize that each group in the painting is distinct from the others and that the groups are divided in a perfectly natural way. Life is treated neither as an instant of time nor as the reflection of light from a given place at that moment, but as a continuous process working in the heart of man. 'Those of the audience who are appreciative are content to perfect the song in their own minds by the force of their own feeling,' as Tagore said. And this fact that the mind is necessary, that it is indeed the main essential in our understanding of nature, is extremely important in Asia.

The logical expression of this idea or attitude is the use of multiple perspective. The Chinese artist often paints landscapes using more than one perspective – sometimes aerial and frontal ones in the same picture. When the intention is simply to record what one person sees from one particular point, then of course the linear or 'scientific' perspective developed in Europe during the Renaissance is the appropriate means of expression. But if the whole conception of a landscape is in the *mind*, then a multiple perspective is natural. In Europe linear perspective was finally rejected by the Cubists, who returned to various forms of the multiple view. Perhaps in this aspect they have something in common with Asian painting.

The spirit or inner tension of all living things was considered by the Chinese more important that any formal likeness. When Hsieh Ho laid down his famous Six Principles of Painting in the fifth century they were based on ideas and traditions which had existed for some time before him. The first and most important of these principles was the 'life movement' and 'the spirit resonance'; not outward appearance but the idea in the mind of the artist and the divine spirit *(ch'i)*, the breath of life or vital rhythm – it was these that had to be revealed by natural form; 'the spirit has no form, yet that which moves and transforms the form is the spirit', said Wang Wei, one of China's greatest landscapists, who lived from 699 to 759. The same underlying principle is also found in Indian art theory, where it is called *pramāna*. 'The source of truth is not empirical perception *(pratyaksha)* but an inwardly known model which at the same time gives form to knowledge and is the cause of knowledge' (Coomaraswamy). Art manifests life, penetrating beneath the surface, revealing the inner nature that lies beyond outward appearance. It is this essential truth which is the cornerstone of Chinese painting.

There is a Taoist saying: 'Only the truly intelligent understand this principle of identity.' But Confucian, Taoist and Buddhist accepted it as self-evident that deep insight, real knowledge of the object, whether man or beast, tree or mountain, were prerequisites for great works of art. These works were apparently accomplished without effort because their secret had been understood before fingers moved the brush.

Although the aim of the artist was to reach perfection – almost divine perfection (when painting has reached divinity, there is an end of the matter) – he was not thought superior to the discipline which governed ordinary man. Though supposed to be 'rich in inner character', he was not idolized as an extraordinary being and was therefore able to understand that rules should be thought of as the vehicle of spontaneity. For the 'activities of man are put forth by conscious effort, consequently the works to be done by man are defined in detail.'

One aspect in which the Chinese civilization differed from others was its early concern with nature. This instinctive feeling for nature, which had not yet found expression in the visual arts, penetrates Chinese literature from the earliest times, reaching its apogee in the poets of the T'ang and Sung epochs and the monochrome landscapes of the Sung artists.

Quite contrary to the attitude prevailing in medieval European literature, as well as in ancient Indian texts, Chinese literature is comparatively devoid of the fear of nature. In the Indian epic, the *Rāmāyana*, a definite terror of the Great Forest is evident, and though the hero, Rama, gives a sensuous description of spring, identifying himself in an idyllic scene with the amorous feeling generated in all living matter, we are very conscious of the dark forest surrounding him and all its attendant horrors. In Europe the northern countries continued to express this fear until quite late

Page 37: Detail of a clay brick, stamped and then fired. Han dynasty. *Mme. Pincket Collection, Brussels.* *Cf. p. 43*

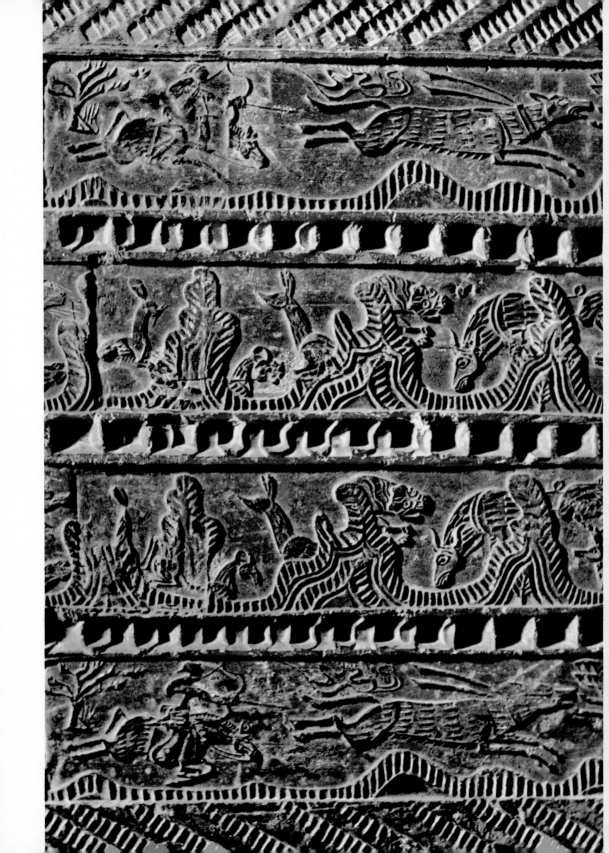

in their history (Clark). The Chinese mind, on the other hand, was surprisingly free from this obsessive fear of the forest, and when the Han painters observed the world about them and the existence of life against its background of landscape, it was the full life of man and his activities that predominated.

Chinese thought, starting from a basis common to most early civilizations, developed in two distinct directions: Taoism and Confucianism. Confucian doctrines were mainly of a social nature, more practical than philosophical. Society was founded on moral law, and filial piety and loyalty to the clan were all-important. For the Confucian man developed best by cultivating specific pursuits such as music, archery, charioteering, calligraphy (which included painting), mathematics and the study of the Five Classics. Taoist philosophy draws a distinction between the material and spiritual worlds and points its own particular way to liberation from the material. The Taoist Ideal Way (Tao) was the life followed by a recluse seeking unity with nature and living in such a manner as to arrive through this at self-knowledge. It was those elements of Taoist thought, and later those of Ch'an (Zen) Buddhism, which provided the spiritual basis for the development of landscape painting. These two currents of thought, the Confucian and the Taoist, the conformist and the speculative, fused. As in India where the abstract metaphysical tendency ran side by side with the pagan and the sensuous, so the two elements in Chinese life, Confucian restraint and the fullness and freedom of Taoism, the one complementing the other, formed the fabric of Chinese culture. These two complementary aspects could be thought of as the ancient ideas of *yin* and *yang*, the male and female principle, dark and light, heart and mind, reason and intuition. 'Painting, guided by the heart-mind *(hsin)*, by means of skilful handling of brush and ink should thus exhibit thought and reflection, sensibility and intuition' (Waley).

Ancient texts give various definitions of *hua*, to paint. The *Kuang*

Page 38: Detail of a hunting relief from Assurbanipal's palace at Nineveh. It depicts very realistically the suffering of the animal, whereas Chinese hunting scenes show a keen feeling for the natural setting. *British Museum. Cf. p. 44*

PLATE P. 195 *Ya* says that it has to do with drawing lines, engraving, depicting. The *Erh Ya* defines *hua* as giving form; and the *Shuo Wên* says it consists in drawing boundaries and the raised paths around the fields. The *Shih Ming* says *hua* is to trace, to lay down the appearance of things with the use of colours. In our plate the Wu-t'ai Shan, one of the sacred Buddhist mountains, is in fact painted in a manner corresponding to the definition laid down in the *Erh Ya;* it is a kind of pictorial map.

Among the main components of Chinese painting which are taken from the art of an earlier period, and now developed and trans-formed, are mountains and streams, clouds and dragons, together with the abstract motifs of early bronzes, lacquer and silk. Of these perhaps the most important is the mountain. *Shan-shui*, literally 'mountains and water', are the Chinese words for landscape painting. And since painting was considered a branch of calligraphy, it is interesting to observe that the characters for mountains, rivers and trees reproduce them pictorially in a simplified graphic form.

The motif of mountains and trees originated in earliest times, and it is traditionally said that among the twelve insignia of the legendary Emperor Shun (2255 B.C. – according to legendary chronology) were the mountain, the dragon and the brightly-coloured bird. The great poet Ch'u Yüan (332–295 B.C.) tells of a princely family shrine in which he saw gods and the spirits of mountain and stream painted on the walls. One of the ancient classics, the Elegies of Ch'u, tells of ancestral temples of early kings and ministers painted with mountains, spirits, sages and monsters. One of the early emperors had his emblems embroidered on his robes and the custom appears to have continued, for in Tun-huang there are some statues with robes that are carved and painted with small landscapes of moun-tains, trees and streams, evidently to depict the actual embroidery on the robes.

It may be argued that these first representations of mountains were only in insignia. But this in itself is revealing, for every civilization has used symbols to represent the factors which it considered vital.

FIG. I – *Motifs: water, river, wood (or tree), forest. Cf. above*

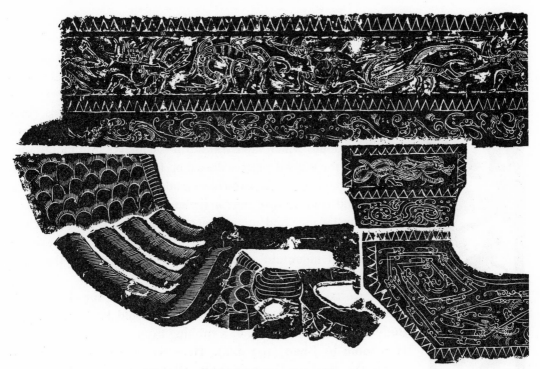

FIG. 2 – *Stone rubbing from a Han tomb recently discovered at I-nan. Cf. p. 42*

The impact of mountains on early Chinese man was an overwhelming one, for mountains were given titles and accorded sacrifices, while legends grew up around them. There were at first five important mountains in China – the Central, the Western, the Northern, the Southern and the Eastern – and of these the most renowned was the Eastern Mountain, or T'ai Shan, which was chosen as the most propitious place for the emperors to sacrifice to Heaven (cf. page 194).

Mountains were thought to be inhabited by Taoist immortals eating from marvellous jade utensils; and the mountains themselves had their own divinities which were equal in rank to the high officials at court. At first they were princes, but during the T'ang dynasty (618–906) they were accorded the title 'Kings of Heaven'.

FIG. 3 – *Funerary urn. Late Chou. Cf. below*

41

Rivers and streams – 'the veins of the earth' – were the channels for life-giving water; the mountain peaks breaking through the clouds brought rain; and rain was a constant preoccupation in China, as in any largely agricultural country. Thus stylized clouds are among the first motifs of ritual bronzes during the Shang dynasty (c. 1500–1050 B.C.). Sometimes clouds are shown as dragons, since the cloud and the dragon were closely associated as humid elements. It is these clouds which later transform themselves into mountains, and one of the earliest sources drawn on for the mountain image in landscape painting is the pre-Han cloud-scroll motif, derived from pottery and from bronze mirror designs. The cloud-scroll appears on silk, on lacquer and metal objects, and quite rapidly develops into primitive but realistic mountain ranges; it is the origin of the 'cloud-tipped mountain' encountered in Tun-huang in the sixth century.

Before we go on to describe the development of the cloud-scroll mountain (already studied by others), it would be interesting to study in greater detail Fig. 2, a rubbing from a recently excavated Han tomb in I-nan (193 B.C.). Here we find various symbolic motifs, the cloud-scroll among them. All these elements – the triangle motif, the scales of the dragon's body, the clouds and the animals are extremely suggestive.

In the accompanying figures we see the development of the cloud-scroll mountain motif. The first example (Fig. 3) is on pottery from the Late Chou period (c. 250 B.C.). Animals are seen around the scroll with a central figure (which might be a shaman dressed up for ritual with appendages of leopards' tails, etc.). This appears to be an early example of rendering animals together with a human figure. Figure 5 is from an inlaid bronze shaft-fitting, also possibly dated to the Late Chou. It is a stylized landscape with the cloud-scroll, still used decoratively but with the conception of a range of hills; in between them are a deer, a dog and a wild boar depicted in full 'flying gallop'. The central scroll builds up into an early form of cone-shaped mountain, and we find a large bird on the

FIG. 4 – *Rubbing from a stone relief. Han dynasty. Sian Museum. Cf. p. 43*

42

FIG. 5 – *Bronze inlaid with gold and silver.*
Cf. pp. 42, 89

summit with a leg on each peak; this motif is also found in the
detail from Cave 285 at Tun-huang. In Figure 5 two tigers close
in on a deer on one of the ridges and another animal is on the
summit of the lower peak. The fine lines may possibly be interpreted
as an effort to depict grass. This is taken a step further in Figure 7
and the plate on p. 37.

Figures 4, 6 and 7 are further developments of the cloud mountain.
The last example has the added interest of architecture, trees,
horsemen and a chariot, while the landscape in the background
includes a range of cloud mountains with animals leaping and
bounding in and out of them. Figures 4 and 7 are rubbings from
newly excavated tomb reliefs in the Sian Museum. In the plate
on p. 37 the mountains are continuous stratified horizontal ranges
with animals appearing from behind the folds; the lower register
has as a background trees and clouds, giving the narrow composition
a sense of space. A huntsman and animals are shown in 'flying
gallop'. In these illustrations we have some of the main elements
essential to early Chinese landscape painting; to these we should
add the mountain with trees along the ridges which also started
in the Late Chou. We see a further development of this on page 92.
The special characteristic of the cloud-scroll lent a wide sweeping

FIG. 6 – *Rubbing from a stone relief. Han dynasty, from Shensi province*

movement to the mountain ranges in early Chinese landscape painting. It has been suggested (Soper) that the Han hunting scene is derived from Scythian and west Iranian origins (cf. plates on pp. 38, 46, 52) and the theme itself may well have come from there; but Scythian and west Iranian art places emphasis on animals (or men and animals) interlocked in combat. More often than not man is shown pitting his strength against beast. It is an actual physical combat more brutal than anything to be found in Han art. The difference between the two artistic concepts is very clear. The one is animal art first and foremost, while the other – Han art – aims at a panoramic landscape even to the extent of primitive stylized technique and execution. Both these tendencies in Han art can be seen in Fig. 8.

The horizontal composition of hills with figures of animals and men weaving in and out, placed like accents in the flow of a melody, is ever-present in Chinese landscape painting. Such a PLATE P. 184 masterpiece as the scroll called 'The Han Emperor entering his capital of Chang-an', in the Boston Museum, exemplifies the highest expression of this harmonious development.

FIG. 7 – *Rubbing from a stone relief. Han dynasty. Cloud-scrolls*

Among the animals the deer is seen more frequently among the earliest cloud-mountains, and all through Han, Wei and Northern Ch'i art – whether it be in stone, lacquer, silk, bronze or paint – it never ceases to appear, bounding in and out of the hills. Indeed the deer is still a symbol of everlasting life and is the only animal able to find the *ling-chih*, the plant of immortality (a kind of edible fungus). Another characteristic early pose is that of an animal sleeping under a tree; we see this in a pre-Han bronze mirror from the Freer Gallery of Art, Washington, and frequently in all periods of Han and Wei art as well as in Tun-huang.

The continuation of these motifs in Chinese art is characteristic. The symbolic linear forms that appear in the Shang bronzes (1500–1050 B.C.) with their original strength and intensity and with all their essentially Chinese quality, were employed over many centuries. As a leit-motif they did not lose their original concept and power with the passing of time and continual usage. The same whirling, dissolving movement of the pre-Han lacquer and bronze design is found again and again in the swirling draperies and scarves

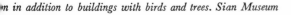

n in addition to buildings with birds and trees. Sian Museum

Shell with hunting scene. The chariot, with archers and charioteer, is shown in a fully frontal view. Late Chou or Early Han period. *Cleveland Museum of Art. Width 8 cm. Cf. p. 44*

of the *apsaras* and other flying figures in the Tun-huang mural paintings and in Wei and T'ang reliefs. The abstract quality of these decorative patterns and of mythical animals and cloud motifs is also continued and finally evolves into the perfect monochrome painting and calligraphy of the Sung dynasty in the tenth and eleventh centuries.

To realize to what extent the abstract swirling line is part of Chinese art one need only look at the *apsaras* of Indian art (whence they PLATE P. 51 came to China). The Indian *apsara* is a sensuous creature with breasts like golden bowls, lotus-eyed, vibrant of flesh. The Chinese is fully clothed, a being of the mind, a spirit, a lute heard in the

FIG. 8 – *Detail of an engraved bronze tube inlaid with gold. Found at Lo-lang. Cf. p. 44*

stillness of twilight. In the T'ang group compositions, however, central figures of the Buddha stand majestically still, while the *apsaras* and the celestial musicians and the nymphs fly headlong into space, their draperies blown by a violent wind. In Chinese art this very wind was one that continued to produce a special rhythm of its own. Wind was thought of as a positive factor in Chinese painting. It was one of the forces of heaven, that stirred things to life; as the wind moved through the trees, over water or around figures, a living quality passed through them, bringing with it the unifying factor of life movement *(shêng-tung)*.

PLATE P. 132

The earliest representation of trees comes from Late Chou times (cf. tree forms, pages 130f.) but pre-Han bronze mirrors associated the tree with the mountain. Here we see its development from pre-Han to T'ang times.

FIGS. 9, 10, 11, 12

Architecture is associated with landscape elements from the Warring States period (480–221 B.C.). These drawings on the bronze basin in Peking show us not only the house, but the auspicious birds on the roof – another recurrent feature of Han art. The same bronze features flowing water with trees and birds; the water is depicted by wavy lines, as are used later on as the *hsi (ch'i) chien hên i fa* – 'rippling waves of shallow water'; they are slightly wavy, approx-

PLATES PP. 64, 149
FIG. 13

FIG. 7

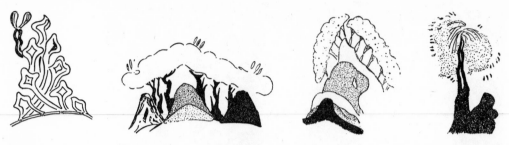

FIGS. 9–12 – *Trees on mountain tops.* FIG. 9 – *A pre-Han bronze mirror.* FIG. 10 – *Wei painting, Tun-huang.* FIG. 11 – *Sui painting, Tun-huang.* FIG. 12 – *T'ang painting, Tun-huang. Cf. p. 47*

FIG. 13 – *Bronze basin. The decoration combines architectural with landscape elements. Cf. p. 47*

48

Polychrome painted tile from a tomb near Lo-yang. Ink and colour on clay. Han period. *Museum of Fine Arts, Boston. Height 19.5 cm. Cf. pp. 58–59, 66*

PLATE P. 171 imately parallel, and occasionally have the form of a sinuous S-curve. We see this technique used in the spring landscape in the T'ang period.

The composition of a certain style of landscape was for centuries influenced by the horizontal composition in registers found on large bronze vessels in early Chinese art. These vessels are decorated PLATES PP. 57, 60 with hunting scenes in flat relief and are referred to as 'hunting bronzes'. The vertical scroll which developed much later was influenced to an equal extent by another indigenous Chinese art FIG. 23 form, calligraphy.

Page 51: Indian *apsara. Musée Guimet, Paris. Cf. p. 46*

Page 52: Panel of a tomb, in fired clay, featuring a hunting scene. Particularly impressive is the way in which movement is represented, of the hunters and of the game. The spirit is entirely different from that of the Assyrian hunting scene on p. 38. Han dynasty. *Museo Nazionale d'Arte Orientale, Rome. Cf. p. 44*

II. THE HAN DYNASTY (206 B.C.–A.D. 220)

The realism and vigour of Han art is the expression of one of the most dynamic periods in China's long history. The dynasty was founded in 206 B.C. by a peasant, Liu Pang, and succeeding emperors attracted to their court many very able men, including writers and poets. Through the system of imperial examinations a competent civil service, recruited regardless of birth, was set up; and thus an official class endowed with leisure – the scholar gentry – was created. It was this class of people, with enough leisure to feel a need for art and who also had the time to create, which was the mainspring of Han vigour in this field.

But it was not only in art that the Han period was remarkable. Imperial universities and provincial schools were set up in 124 B.C.; the first assembly of scholars gathered in A.D. 4, and other assemblies were called from time to time to discuss such matters as constitutional law and the nationalization of the salt and iron industries. There was a renaissance of Confucianism, and at the same time Taoist thought developed to a considerable extent. The growth of sceptical and rational ideas liberated the minds of men from many past superstitions. Astronomers perfected their instruments and invented new ones. The waterclock now measured time for an entire day (Maspero). And in 52 B.C. the emperor was presented by Shên Hsiu-ch'ang with an instrument which 'permitted him to measure the movement of the sun and moon and to verify the form and movement of the sky' (Needham). Ink had been in use before Han times, but now took on added importance with the invention of paper and improvements made in the manufacture of the brush; and this led in turn to the development of painting on silk and paper.

It was a time of tremendous intellectual questioning: books were written on the classics, on medicine, agriculture, military science, history, linguistics, folk literature, philosophy, divination, astronomy, alchemy, botany and zoology. They were, however, still written on bamboo or other wooden strips and on silk, for paper was considered an inferior material.

With these developments in knowledge came economic expansion. Mercantile initiative opened up the Silk Road across the Central Asian desert, linking China with India, Iran and Syria; it was by this route that Buddhism reached China in A.D. 65, as did Roman and Syrian embassies from the West. The first Han envoy Chang Ch'ien left in the middle of the second century B.C. New plants and natural products, alfalfa, grapes, oranges, lemons and jade from Khotan were brought back by these diplomatic missions. The simultaneous developments in ceramics (proto-porcelain) and glazes on decorated tiles and bricks, together with the creation of an advanced textile industry, give a picture of a strong expanding economy (Needham).

PLATE P. 151
BELOW

The empire gradually spread to Central Asia and Korea. Trade flourished and the superior techniques of the imperial armies were disseminated among the more backward neighbours of the Middle Kingdom.

Han poetry reflects this expansion. It is filled with the sorrow of separation, the agonized cry of the soldier long exiled from his home and of the lover pining for his beloved.

> On the field of battle
> There is no date for our reunion,
> Deep sighs, hands press hands,
> Heavy tears of farewell.
> Keep your youth,
> Do not forget the time of our joy.
> Living I shall see you again,
> Dead I shall think of you eternally . . .[1]

But mingled inextricably with the more material aspects of Han times were other less factual concepts: *yin* and *yang*, which from earliest times epitomized the male and female principles, and were

---

[1] Based upon a translation by E. Chavannes.

54

FIG. 14 – *Salt Wells of Tsê-liu ching. Stamped brick. Han dynasty. Cf. pp. 56f.*

equated with light and dark, heaven and earth, hardness and softness; and *wu-hsing*, the Five Elements of wood, fire, earth, metal and water. These ancient ideas and the theories connected with them permeated the art as well as the thought of the Han people. The artist considered that correct representation of the Two Forces and Five Elements brought happiness and prosperity 'and one might be allowed to visit the land of the immortals and to enter Heaven riding a flying dragon or a floating cloud.'

In Han art, as in reality, everyday life proceeded without constraint in this realm of pure fantasy, and each was of equal importance to the creative artist. In his mind the myths and the creatures that figured in them were still very real, and the intermingling of the real and the mythical evidently had a special attraction for him.

It was perhaps a new problem and prompted the scholar poet and painter Chang Hêng (A.D. 78–139) to comment on the general preference of artists for demons and monsters as their subjects. 'Real objects are difficult to represent, but the realm of the unreal is infinite.'[2] Another author asks: 'Why do artists take delight in painting demons and spiritual beings and dislike painting dogs and horses? Is it because the former never appear in reality and the latter are objects of our daily experience?'[3] But even at this stage the tendency was not towards mere imitation of reality for the same author goes on to say: 'When form is laboured the spirit is dissipated, and an artist with too much regard for detail spoils his work.'

Han painting appears to have been mainly mural, although hempen cloth and silk were also thought suitable as surfaces. But until a few years ago historians of Chinese art had very little evidence of pre-Han and Han painting, and they quite correctly assumed that there was a close stylistic resemblance between the painting of the period and the stamped bricks and low reliefs found on the walls of Han tombs. This inference was borne out by ancient texts containing descriptions of frescoes in palaces and temples. No other country in the world has such a vast literature by painters and critics, some of them from very early periods. Now, thanks to the work being done by Chinese archaeologists and historians (especially on Han and pre-Han excavations), knowledge of these times is being deepened, modified and perfected. The tomb paintings found in Manchuria and Liao-yang and hundreds of newly discovered stamped bricks, many of them with landscape elements, constitute a whole fresh field of material for study.

FIGS. 14, 15, 16 In Figures 14–16 representative examples of Han landscapes are

[2] *The Spirit of the Brush*, tr. Shio Sakanishi, London, 1939, p. 21.
[3] Ibid., pp. 19–20.

Page 57: Typical example of a so-called 'hunting bronze'. These vessels are decorated with hunting scenes in bas-relief, arranged in horizontal registers. Warring States period (4th–3rd centuries B.C.). *Pillsbury Collection, Minneapolis Museum. Height 35.2 cm. Cf. p. 50*

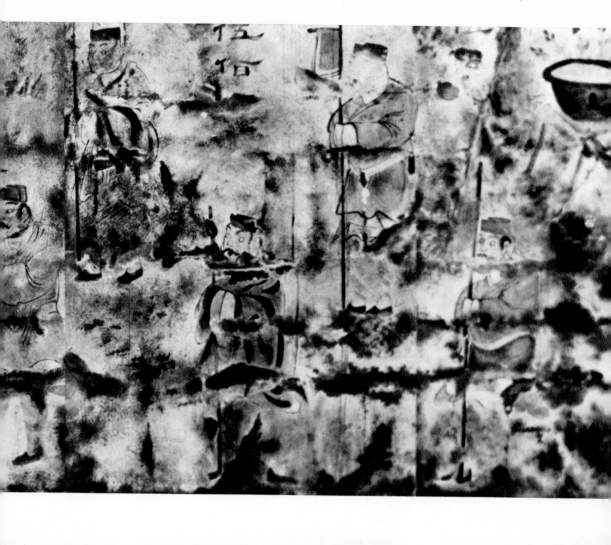

given which form a further development of the earlier ones with the cloud-scrolls (Figs. 4–7).

Landscape elements are seen in a variety of forms. The stamped bricks are generally of two different types (Medley). The first are PLATE P. 52 the pure hunting scenes, with hardly any landscape elements; these no doubt are influenced by Syrian and Iranian hunting themes. Others are well-developed landscape scenes. Three of them are shown here: Fig. 14 represents the salt wells at Tsê-liu ching; Figure 15 represents duck-hunting and harvesting; Fig. 16 a lake FIG. 15 covered with lotus buds and leaves on which a boat is sailing, while FIG. 16 the projecting range of hills with trees behind them completes the scene. Both these landscapes are extraordinary manifestations of popular feeling for nature, for the stamped bricks are genuine expressions of popular art. Here, as it were, is the root of the matter; the feeling for nature comes, not only from intellectuals writing poetry and consciously striving to identify themselves with their surroundings; not only from Taoist philosophy, where man's unity with nature leads him to self-knowledge; but from the people, the craftsmen in the small towns and villages. Only a craftsman who possessed a deep love of nature could do these landscape scenes. In the scene of the Salt Wells the build-up of the Mountains FIG. 14 is in the same spirit as that which conceived the landscape of the plates on pages 152 and 149 from the T'ang period at Tun-huang. Below on the left is the shaft of the Salt Well with four figures working in it; a bridge leads up from the mouth of the well over the intervening space to the place where the salt is poured into pans over a furnace, tended by a figure sitting beside it. Two men with

Pages 58–59 above: Detail of a fresco in a tomb, Hopei province. The style resembles that of the painted tile shown on p. 49. *Peking Museum. Cf. p. 66*

Pages 58–59 below: Partridge, rabbit and pheasant. Detail of a fresco in a tomb, Hopei province. *Cf. p. 66*

Page 60: Detail of the vase shown on p. 57. *Peking Museum*

FIG. 15 – *Duck-hunting and harvesting. Stamped brick from a tomb. Late Han dynasty. Ch'eng-tu Collection (private). Cf. p. 61*

baskets on their backs move across the hills beyond the bridge. The rest of the composition is taken up by wooded hills with animals and birds bounding over them, within the spatial units created by the surface of each mountain. The perspective is no different from that which we will encounter in nearly all our land-scapes, but is only in an earlier phase; *ti*, earth, is all important, and *t'ien*, heaven, is not correlated to the earth – in other words, the horizon line is not present.

FIG. 16 In the scene of the lake with the boat, the lotus, the ducks, the hills and the trees make a landscape that is the forerunner of all those innumerable nostalgic paintings of later periods where a solitary figure in a boat drifts down the water. Can we not hear the Sung

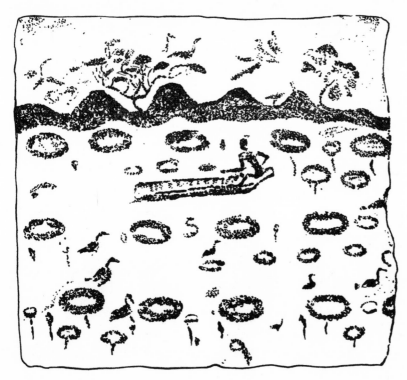

FIG. 16 – *Boat on a lake with lotus-blossoms. Stamped brick. Han dynasty. Cf. pp. 61, 62, 64*

poets a thousand years later singing 'the mist rising from the water hides the mountains' or 'there is no human sound in any direction, there is noise among the trees. It is the sound of autumn.'

The trees used in the Salt Wells of Tsê-liu ching are the cold forest, or *han-lin*, variety, trees without leaves, used first in the bronze basin in Figure 13 and in our T'ang landscape in the plate on FIG. 13 page 171. It is not a matter of their being ignorant how to draw trees with leaves; in the same bronze basin we get a willow-tree. But the two main types of tree were the *han-lin* type without leaves and the *mao-lin* type with them. We get both of them from the Warring States period throughout Chinese painting, the Han period being no exception. Incidentally these bricks are polychrome, a PLATE P. 64

63

Painted clay tile. The pattern, showing a horse, geese and a tree, is continuous; the way in which the trees are rendered is interesting. Han period. *Museum of Fine Arts, Boston. Cf. p. 63*

fact which brings them nearer the category of painting and drawing than that of relief.

In these stamped bricks the perspective varies; sometimes animal and human figures are larger than the mountains, while at other times, as in the Salt Wells and the Boat on the Lake, and in the line drawing in Figure 19 there is a distinct capacity to apprehend man and the universe around him. The setting of the hills with diagonal lines in the Salt Wells does give the effect of depth, while foreshortening of the figure is seen in many of these stamped bricks. It seems to be quite a familiar device, for it is also used in the stone engraving in Figure 19, where the seated figures are treated admirably, while in the boat scene in Figure 16 it is handled with some degree of assurance. In this exquisite scene of the Boat on the Lake the feeling for space is remarkable. The solitary figure of the boatman is in the act of rowing, and the sense of distance between him in his boat and the distant mountains is cleverly conveyed. The two trees placed between the folds of the peaks and the birds flying in the sky accentuate the sense of distance. The duck-hunting scene,

FIG. 19

FIG. 17 – *Battle on the bridge. Rubbing from a stone panel. From the tomb of Wu Liang-tz'ŭ, Shantung province.* A.D. *147–168*

which has often been reproduced, is one of the most beautiful early examples of landscape anywhere in the world.

Stone reliefs are another important source material for the study of Han art. Scenes from mythology, court ceremonies, processions and hunting scenes are usually linear in design, with the figures in profile as in early Egyptian engravings. Figure 19 originates from newly excavated tombs.

Architectonic elements are used in nearly all Han stone reliefs. In the Wu family tomb, a great concourse of figures are arranged behind each other in recessive planes within an architectural frame. This early representation seems to forecast the grandiose development of the T'ang paradise scenes at Tun-huang with tier upon tier of Buddhist personages or, as Arthur Waley puts it, 'the back-benchers of the Buddhist pantheon'. The line drawings in Figures 17, 18 and 20 are from the Wu family tomb; the other, Figure 21, FIGS. 17, 18, 20, 21 is a stamped brick from Szechwan and shows a dwelling surrounded by a wall and divided into two courts, both of which are flanked by wooden verandahs. There is a single-storey structure with three bays and a pitched roof with gable ends. The right-hand area has

65

a well, wooden racks for drying clothes and a kitchen. The high tower with a roof supported on brackets may be a watch-tower. It is probably the dwelling of a rich merchant. The perspective used here is basically the same as that in the T'ang dynasty, as for example in Cave 217.

PLATE P. 155

PLATES PP. 58, 59

PLATE P. 49

These details from a fresco in a tomb in Hopei province show an important style in Han painting, a style similar to that of the famous Han painted bricks in the Boston Museum. The figures carry offerings for the dead and are arranged according to rank. The frieze below contains a partridge, a rabbit and a pheasant.

FIG. 18 – *Abode in the clouds. Rubbing from a stone panel. From the rear chamber of the tomb of Wu Liang-tz'ŭ, Shantung province.* A.D. *147–168*

The uniting factor in the composition, that which holds the figures together, is the element of space. It is not a mere emptiness but a positive agent. The feeling for space as a positive rather than a negative element is one of the continuing characteristics of Chinese painting. The poet Su Tung-p'o in the eleventh century remarks on this when talking of a painting by Wu Tao-tzŭ: 'There was life even in the places where the brush had not reached.'

The Tao abides in emptiness, it is said – and in the Chuang-tzŭ (300 B.C.) importance is given to non-being or emptiness: 'One should not listen with one's ears but with the mind, and not with the mind but with the spirit. The Spirit is an emptiness ready to receive all things' (Waley). The great painter is able to occupy his mind not only with the part of the surface that is filled with the brush and ink, but also with that part from which brush and ink are absent; whoever can understand how this absence is realized can attain a divine quality in his painting. Thus space is like a musical pause, filled with mystery before the next phrase begins, giving it meaning and uniting it with what went before.

For these frescoes a fluid brush-line defines the upper part of the bodies of animals and birds, while a fine incised line is used for human figures. Both the broad fluid stroke and the fine incised line stem from Neolithic times: the first was used in the decoration FIG. 22 of prehistoric painted pottery, while the second is reminiscent of early calligraphy incised on bones with a stylus of some kind. FIG. 23

In the excellent museum at Sian in Shensi province there is an outstanding example of a lacquered bronze mirror. It is about twenty-five centimetres in diameter and painted with a landscape. A group of nobles are conversing under the trees while their horses and grooms stand by. The colours are green, scarlet and yellow on a black ground. The composition is circular, following the shape of the mirror itself. It is one of the earliest examples of Han painted landscape, though with the amount of research now in progress more may come to light. Unfortunately we are unable to reproduce this object and therefore refer to a shell bearing painted hunting PLATE P. 46 scenes. Somewhat earlier in date, it consists of two such scenes each of which contains identical elements such as birds in flight.

FIG. 19 – *Rubbing from a recently discovered stone p*

FIG. 20 – *Rubbing from a stone panel. From the tomb of Wu Liang-tz'ŭ. According to Chavannes the secoɴ register shows the god of thunder in his chariot, drawn by six men*

68

figures are out of scale with the mountains. Han dynasty

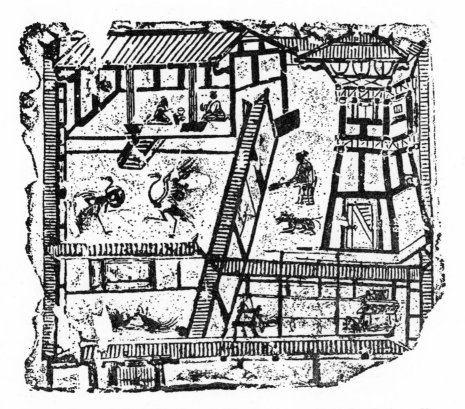

FIG. 21 – *Courtyard with dwelling-house. Rubbing from a stamped brick from Szechwan. Han dynasty. Cf. p. 65*

FIG. 22 – *Neolithic pot. Musée Cernuschi, Paris*

In Han times, however, the artist's feeling for nature often far outstripped his capacity to express it in visual media. Even in the fourth century the artist Tsung Ping, obsessed as he was with painting mountains, was at the same time struggling with primary problems of technique. But the essence of the feeling that permeated the Han artist in general is evident in the period's main characteristics – line and movement as vigorous and bold as the era itself. The love of natural beauty in men's minds was still like a lotus bud arising out of deep waters and waiting for the time when it could open out in all its glory. The great poets who could sing their hymns to nature were still to come.

> The chain of mountain extends a hundred *li*,
> Their peaks pierce the clouds;
> Below the sinuous river winds its way,
> The trees bend their tortuous branches,
> The rain obscures the sky.
> In search of lonely paths I walk along a river
> Whose source I cannot reach,
> The return path is lost in the distance . . .[4]
>
> > *Ssŭ T'iao*
> > (6th century A.D.)

Such a sentiment was unfamiliar to the Han spirit. The group of nobles conversing under the tree in the lacquer landscape were quite possibly enjoying the beauties of nature, but only, one feels, during a pause on their journey somewhere, when they have taken a moment's respite from activity. They do not identify themselves with the landscape; at any moment one of them will leap on to his horse and join the eternal procession of galloping Han cavaliers. The time when man desired to escape to a 'crystal stream that

---

[4] Based upon a translation by E. Chavannes.

flows around a headland as green as jade severed from the dusty world,' where he could 'brush the dust of the town from his clothes and choose a place surrounded by tumbling hills' – that moment was still far away. Yet it was again Tsung Ping who in the fourth century lamented, 'now I am old and infirm I fear I shall no more be able to roam among the beautiful mountains . . . I meditate on the mountain trails and wander only in dreams. As I pluck my lute, multitudinous mountains shall stir the air and echo my songs... As to landscapes, they have a material aspect but also a spiritual influence . . . I can only do my pictures and spread my colours over the cloud-covered mountain to transmit for future ages the hidden meaning which lies beyond all description in words.'[5]
Though the Egyptians and Greeks did have landscapes in their art, in the West the profound appreciation of landscape as such arose very much later than it did in China, and it was only in the fourteenth century that Petrarch, writing to a friend, could say, 'Would that you know with what joy I wander free and alone among mountains and forest.'

[5] Based upon a translation by E. Chavannes.

Page 73: Kneeling archer taking aim at some birds. Ku K'ai-chih was one of the greatest painters at the court of Nanking in the 4th century. This detail of a scroll ascribed to him is reminiscent of the wall-painting in Cave 285 at Tun-huang (p. 74). *British Museum. Cf. p. 84*

Page 74: This detail of the plate (pp. 94–95) from Cave 285 (A.D. 538–539) calls to mind a scroll ascribed to the famous painter Ku K'ai-chih, now in the British Museum. *Cf. pp. 73, 89*

III. THE THREE KINGDOMS
AND THE SIX DYNASTIES (A.D. 220–589)

> They (the ancient pictures) had their origin in forms,
> (the forms) were made to blend with the spirit and
> to excite the heart-mind. If the spirit has no percep-
> tion of them, they exercise no influence; the eyes can
> see only the limits, but not the whole thing ... To
> work at autumn clouds makes the soul soar as a bird,
> to feel the wind of spring makes the thoughts go far
> and wide ... to exert oneself with strange mountains
> and seas, with green forests and the soaring wind,
> with the foaming waters and the rushing cascades –
> how wonderful![1]
>
> *Wang Wei*
> (A.D. 699–759)

The period immediately following the disintegration of the powerful
Han Empire takes its name from the Three Kingdoms into which
the country was divided (A.D. 220–265). These years of internal
chaos, peasant revolts and civil wars generally reduced and im-
poverished the population.

The partition of China continued during the three-hundred-year
rule of the Six Dynasties until the end of the sixth century, when
the country was again united under the Sui rulers.

During the third and fourth centuries China suffered repeatedly
from the attacks of Tibetans, Turco-Mongols, Huns and proto-
Mongols. The lawful dynasty took refuge in the south, and Nanking
became until late in the sixth century the capital of the ruling
dynasties. The isolation of the southern dynasties, cut off from the
rest of the country, created the need for and developed the importance of such maritime cities as Canton and Chiao-chih.

A great number of Buddhist missionaries from India frequented

---

[1] O. Sirén, *The Chinese on the Art of Painting*, Peking, 1936, p. 17.

This cave has many elements from the tradition of the Han stone reliefs. A third wall which we are not able to reproduce here has exactly the same architectural structure as reliefs from the tomb of the Han general Ho Ch'ü-ping in the Wei river valley in Shensi. The illustrations show parts of the *Ruru Jātaka*, the story of the golden deer king, who while crossing a river one day saved the life of a drowning man by helping him ashore. The man knelt down and thanked the beautiful deer. The queen of Benares dreamed of a deer with nine colours and implored the king to get her his skin for a dress and his horns for drinking-cups. The king gave the command, and the man whom the deer had saved came and told the king where he could be found. The deer was asleep but a swallow who was his friend came and awoke him to the danger. The deer met the king and told him the story of his betrayal.

The *Ruru Jātaka* is rarely represented in art and this is perhaps the only time it was shown in the Wei period. It has been suggested that the red ground and the plants scattered over the surface are due to the influence of fourth-century Sassanian art. But we saw this tendency in the Han funerary slab (Plate p. 52). As for the red ground, which enriches and enhances the surface quality of the painting, it is an exact description from the *Jātaka* itself. When the king asks the treacherous man 'Where is the golden deer?', he replies, 'Within yonder clump of flowering sal and mango, where the ground is all as red as cochineal, this deer is to be found.' It is also interesting to note that the earth of northern India around Benares and Delhi is deep red ochre, in fact an astonishing colour. The painter was obviously following the description in the *Jātaka*.

The line here expresses strength rather than movement. The saw-toothed hills leading down from left to right bring us into the heart of the forest clearing. We can somehow sense the spiritual quality of the future Buddha in the guise of the animal: he stands unafraid, above the meanness of man, detached, in supreme awareness, entirely sure of his destiny. The man is shown dark-skinned and wearing a *dhoti* (Indian male dress) – obviously an Indian, as the story takes place in India. *Cf. pp. 79, 81*

CAVE 257

this maritime route to China. In A.D. 520, during the reign of Liang Wu-ti, the legendary Bodhidharma, founder of the Ch'an (Zen) Buddhist sect (which later greatly influenced landscape painting), arrived at Canton and was personally welcomed by the emperor Wu, himself a devout Buddhist.

In the north the military conflicts with various tribes continued to sow chaos and misery until the arrival on the scene of the victorious Turco-Mongol T'o-pa, who not only conquered but stabilized the northern territories. These invaders, soon to be known as the Northern Wei, were themselves quickly assimilated and became completely 'sinicized'.

The Buddhist missionaries and monks of Tun-huang played an important role during these troubled times, and under their civilizing influence the Northern Wei became the first great imperial patrons of Buddhist art in China. For over two centuries they encouraged and took an active part in the building of thousands of temples and in the hewing of caves.

Their first capital was at P'ing-Ch'êng not far from Peking, but by the middle of the fifth century they had gained control of north China, and in A.D. 494 established their capital at Lo-yang in the Yellow River basin.

In the fourth century Tun-huang, which until then had been spared from external disturbances, fell under Northern Wei control. The emperor moved thirty-nine thousand of its inhabitants to P'ing-Ch'eng. This was of major importance to the arts, for these people comprised craftsmen and sculptors, and it was with their help that the Yün-kang caves were begun. The cave-temples of Yün-kang were started in A.D. 414 and those of Lung-mên at the end of the same century. These caves contain examples of some of the greatest religious sculpture ever produced anywhere in the world.

In the enthusiasm evoked by their recent conversion, the Wei rulers spent enormous sums of money on their temples; the height of their fervour as builders was reached under Hsien-wên Ti (466–471),

CAVE 257. Detail of plate on p. 77

his son and the dowager Empress Wu (515–528). This empress engaged thousands of men to work on the Lung-mên caves, and cut down the salaries of officials in order to maintain the temples. She built the Monastery of Eternal Peace at Lo-yang and a pagoda said to have been a thousand feet high. The heavy expenditures and taxation necessary for the realization of these grandiose projects soon rendered the empress Wu highly unpopular. This general discontent became so great that, even after she had retired into a nunnery in 528, she was taken out and assassinated by rebels.

During the Six Dynasties Confucianism, neo-Taoism and Buddhism flourished side by side and the resultant compound of these three modes of thought was of particular intellectual interest. This fusion is clearly illustrated in the poetic works of T'ao Yüan-ming (A.D. 365–427). A Confucian by upbringing, Taoism inspired him and Buddhism deeply penetrated his spirit as he sang of nature, of abandoned fields, of the escape to be found in wine, and distant hamlets faintly seen in the mist.

While the poetry of the Six Dynasties reflects all three tendencies, it is especially the neo-Taoist spirit that dominates the attitude towards nature. Yüan Chi in the third century was perhaps the first poet to develop the theme of man lost in the immensity of nature which later inspired T'ang and Sung poets and painters. Most popular were such themes as distant vistas of landscape lost in the mist, the cries of birds announcing dawn, the first rays of the sun piercing the clouds, the rose light of morning over flowers, and Taoist immortals dwelling on mountain heights.

Love poems became increasingly frequent, and such images as sweet-scented women with vermilion lips and long hands as smooth as jade playing soft music, bathed in a delicate romantic spirit, heralded the T'ang and Sung. At the same time epic poems, in the tradition of heroic literature, tell us of heroines such as Mu-lan donning man's attire and fighting the northern invaders.

The art of the Six Dynasties is both a continuation of the Han and a transition to the T'ang. From this period poetry and painting came closer and closer in spirit until in the tenth and eleventh centuries, during the Sung, each was indeed a reflection of the other.

CAVE 257 (A.D. 386–532)

The Buddha is here seated in a cove within a rocky landscape, while before him kneels a new disciple whose head is being shaved by a monk. A noble figure, standing in devotion, watches the scene. This majestic composition is one of the finest paintings at Tun-huang. It is a triumph of harmony and structure with a silent inner strength that calls to mind Piero della Francesca.

CAVE 428 (*c.* 520–530. Late Wei). Pages 85, 93 above

The *Mahāsattva Jātaka*. Three brothers bid farewell to their father and engage in some target practice before going out hunting. At the sight of a starving tigress and her cubs Mahāsattva invents some pretext to be alone, and when the others ride away lies down in front of the tigress so that she may have food. But the pitiful animal has no strength to eat him. He goes to the top of the hill and, using a sharp bamboo stick, pierces his throat and falls down in front of her. The brothers return to find Mahāsattva dead, they build a *stūpa* for him and return to tell their father. The last scene is Mahāsattva reborn as the Buddha.

The narrative composition in horizontal registers follows the tradition of the 'hunting bronzes'. The same characters are repeated as the story unfolds and the action takes place within the clearly divided 'space cells' defined by the 'saw-toothed' hills and trees. Depth is here suggested by the overlapping of elements: by horsemen and figures appearing from behind a hill; by foreshortening, as when a horse and rider are seen from the front; and by oblique lines, to suggest recession. The stylized trees of the Han period begin to change and take on the aspect of identifiable species. The general organization has now surpassed that of the simplified Han reliefs. The scenes where Mahāsattva throws himself over the cliff and where the brothers return show a distinctly new sense of perspective and depth. The same cave has the *Suddhanta Jātaka* and the Temptation of the Buddha by the Demon Māra.

82

In this period the evolution of criticism and aesthetic theory developed. The Six Principles formulated by Hsieh Ho, painter and theoretician, were intended as standards for the evaluation of painting. 'Which are these Six Principles? The first is spirit resonance (or vibration of vitality) and life movement. The second is bone-manner (i.e., structural) use of the brush. The third is, to conform with the objects to give likeness. The fourth is, to apply the colours according to the characteristics. The fifth is plan and design, place and position (i.e., composition). The sixth is, to transmit models by drawing.'[2]

The subject-matter of Chinese painting was divided into ten groups. A twelfth-century catalogue of the Sung emperor Hui-tsung's collection classifies subjects as follows:

1. *Tao-shih:* religious subject
2. *Jên-wu:* human affairs
3. *Kung-shih:* palaces and other buildings
4. *Fan-tsu:* foreign tribes
5. *Lung-yu:* dragons and fishes
6. *Shan-shui:* landscapes or mountains and streams
7. *Ch'in-shou:* animals
8. *Hua-niao:* flowers and birds
9. *Mo-chu:* bamboos in ink
10. *Su-kuo:* vegetables and fruit.

The importance of each group was based on ancient tradition whereby painting 'served as a moral guide'. It was natural that the first category, *Tao-shih*, should be devoted to religious subjects, mainly Taoist and Buddhist.

[2] Ibid., pp. 30–1.

Incidentally it is interesting to note the remarks of Chang Yen-yüan, the T'ang dynasty critic, 'There are still some famous pictures handed down from the Wei and the Chin dynasties and I have had occasion to see them. The landscapes are filled with crowded peaks; their effect is like that of filigree ornaments or horn combs. The views are generally enclosed by trees and rocks which stand in a circle on the ground; they look like rows of lifted arms with outspread fingers.' *Cf. pp. 85, 93*

Religious themes fall into three main divisions:

1. Purely religious figures of Buddha and all the numerous lesser personages, and paradise scenes.
2. The Jātaka tales (stories of the Buddha's former lives) and scenes depicting the life of the Buddha.
3. Scenes from the lives of saints, famous monks and teachers, and portraits of donors.

The two last-mentioned groups gave scope for secular scenes as well as landscape painting, which gradually invaded the temporal scenes of Buddhist painting until during the Late T'ang it dominated all other subjects. It is curious to note, however, that even as late as the twelfth century it was thought morally correct to give landscape

PLATE P. 73 only sixth place.

Perhaps the greatest artist of the Nanking court in the fourth and beginning of the fifth century was Ku K'ai-chih, one of the earliest painters of Buddhist themes. He is recorded as having painted some three hundred frescoes on the walls of temples and palaces in Ch'ang-an and Lo-yang, but few examples of his work have come down to us. It is said that when he painted human figures he let several years pass before painting the eyes, for, he explained, 'The features can be beautiful or ugly. They are not very important beside the mysterious parts by which the soul is expressed in a portrait.' He painted a famous contemporary musician among rocks, for 'he is a man who must be seen in a landscape of mountains.'[3]

He is best known to us by virtue of a scroll attributed to him which is now in the British Museum. One of the panels in this scroll has a
PLATE P. 73 landscape scene with a kneeling archer shooting at animals, with a mountain in the middle of the composition. A detail from Cave 285 done in A.D. 538 shows an almost identical scene.

[3] Ibid., p. 12.

CAVE 428

Detail of the plate on p. 82 (Cave 428) containing the two scenes in which Mahāsattva sacrifices himself to the starving tigress.

The Han world of *yin* and *yang* is still able to inspire the artist. Whirling, dissolving arabesques contain celestial beings mounted on many-headed dragons and mythical figures, half bird and half man, spreading their strong wings and soaring into the clouds, while below the earth is represented by strange mountains. Into this imaginary and fabulous world are suddenly introduced realistic and vividly rendered drawings – an ox, a sow and her litter – seemingly odd intruders; but for the Chinese this combination of real and unreal is identical with heaven and earth, dark and light – the male and female *yin-yang* concept of the universe. It has the spirit of Han art, one of whose essential qualities is that the realm of pure fantasy continues to ignore all boundaries between the imaginary and the real. This spirit figure riding on the clouds and the phoenix (Fig. 24) from a Han lacquer painting in Changsha belong to the same dual world as the frescoes in Cave 249; the bird-man figure (Plate p. 87 above) has its counterpart in a Han stone relief (Fig. 18), as does the many-headed dragon (Plate p. 88 below, Fig. 25).

FIG. 24 – *A spirit riding on the clouds. Han dynasty*

The detail from Cave 285 is still very close in spirit to the earlier Han style, while in the Ku K'ai-chih scroll spatial treatment is PLATE P. 74 further developed. In both works we find the same Han 'cone-shaped' mountains and the relative proportion and disposition of elements is almost identical in the two paintings. In our details we find the eagle on top of the cone-shaped mountain as we find one sitting on the summit of the cloud-mountain in the encrusted metal box in the Warring States period (Fig. 5). On the Ku K'ai-chih FIG. 5 scroll the following maxim accompanies the landscape:

'In the eternal movement of the world there is nothing which is exalted that is not afterwards brought low; among living things there is none which having attained its apogee, does not thenceforth decline. When the sun has reached the middle of its course, it begins to sink: when the moon is full, it is on the way to wane. We are raised up as on a crumbling heap of dust; we fall with shock as sudden as the rebound of a tense spring.'[4]

Sir Kenneth Clark mentions a similar theme in the Canterbury Psalter (Usquequo Domine) and the Utrecht Psalter.

Composition, or chang-fa, was the suitable filling-in of space. Kuo COMPOSITION AND Hsi says that whenever one is going to use the brush one must PERSPECTIVE correlate sky and earth ... between them one may develop the ideas of scenery. 'In placing objects in relation to one another the first step was t'ien-ti, heaven and earth, that is the placing of the horizon line.'[5] Some artists have both t'ien and ti; others one and not the other, so that the relative importance of the blank spaces at the top and bottom of a picture was a primary consideration. The balance between solid forms and empty spaces, hsiu shih, the balance between large and small forms, the pi chi or 'guest and host' principle, and ch'iu ho or spaciousness were perhaps the most

[4] L. Binyon, Admonitions of the Instructress in the Palace, London, 1912, p. 17.
[5] B. March, Some Technical Terms of Chinese Painting, Baltimore, 1935, paras. 155–8.

Page 88: CAVE 249. Cf. p. 86

FIG. 25 – *Many-headed dragon. Stone relief. Han dynasty. Cf. lower plate on p. 88*

important elements, for 'a painting has or lacks *ch'iu ho* just as the artist has it or lacks it in his heart, and a single man may fill a picture with three strokes and good composition. Another with poor composition will never attain success, no matter how many strokes he uses.'[6]

The space relation was never solved harshly; one element blended into the other, and the differentiation between the groups in a composition are only those of life itself. Never an arbitrary line or rigid square, never the rectangle of a dividing frame: a group of trees, some rocks, the walls of a pavilion, a range of mountains, a river or lake – these are the only divisions which, while defining the composition, may all be integrated into a complete landscape. Action takes place within natural boundaries and remains 'faithful to its own structure'.

The viewpoint from which a landscape was painted was not a fixed one as in scientific perspective; as already mentioned in the second

[6] Ibid., paras. 155, 160.

90

FIG. 26 – *An example of 'kao-yüan' or 'high distance'. After a painting ascribed to Tung Yüan (947–970). Cf. p. 104*

chapter, it was in the form of what we may call multiple perspective – that is to say, each element in the landscape was seen from a different perspective, so that when, as was generally the case, a landscape was seen from an elevated point of view (bird's-eye view), it still allowed a frontal view of objects.

As the viewpoint is mobile, and parallel lines do not converge towards a vanishing-point but remain parallel (architectural details), the result is a feeling of panoramic immensity, a sense of movement and participation. One is looking at the scene as from a slight eminence, in detachment, and yet simultaneously wandering through it.

The following poem, 'Mount Lu', is a good description of the state of mind in which a Chinese landscape should be appreciated. Here Mount Lu represents 'the World of Happening and Being'.

> From that side it seems a peak
> From this side a range,
> View it from on high, view it from below
> It is never twice the same –
> How comes it that we cannot know
> This mountain's real form?
> It is, oh friend, it is that we
> Are dwellers on the Mount of Lu.[7]   *Su Tung-p'o*

[7] A. Waley, *An Introduction to the Study of Chinese Painting*, London, 1923, p. 177.

CAVE 428 (*c.* A.D. 520–530. Late Wei). Pages 82, 93 above and 96

Page 93 above: This plate is an enlargement of the coloured plate on p. 82 (Mahāsattva panel). It illustrates one of the best-known Jātakas, dealing with the early incarnations of Śakyamuni; in this, by his wisdom and boundless self-sacrifice, frequently in animal guise, Śakyamuni gradually acquires such a good karma that during his final incarnation he can become the Buddha. Here this Jātaka is illustrated scene by scene in three long panels. We see the three brothers, the sons of a prince, setting out for the hunt; finding in a ravine a starving tiger with its cubs; the youngest brother, Mahāsattva ('the great being'), jumping off a cliff in compassion, being devoured by tigers, and finally, after his two other brothers have reported this to their father and erected a stūpa to commemorate the deceased, he appears to them as a perfect Buddha. This painting, though still archaic in style, occupies an important place in art history for two reasons: because it is a lively, almost dramatic narrative of a theme significant in Buddhist ethics, and because the scenes are set in a landscape which both divides and links them.

Page 93 below.

Some examples of animals 'in the flying gallop' are featured on the Han stone relief (A.D. 114) from Ch'ing-ping Hsien, Shantung. Also of particular interest is the rendering of a horse 'in the flying gallop' (Plate p. 93 above).

In Chinese art dogs, deer, hares and a boar are seen in this position, which seems to have come about in 400 B.C. (Plate p. 93 below). In Europe although it appeared in Mycenaean times, it occurs but rarely; one instance is in a drawing by Leonardo da Vinci dated A.D. 1485. Many European scholars have written about the *galop volant*, and it seems that it suddenly became popular in the eighteenth century as a result of Chinese influence. Degas uses it, for instance, in painting his horses. The slow-motion camera shows us that in fact this position does not actually occur in galloping but only in jumping. Dr Chêng Tê-k'un thinks that the horse and other animals seen in this position in Chinese art are meant to be jumping and not galloping, as they are generally depicted over projecting peaks and other obstacles.

Von der Heydt Collection, Rietberg Museum, Zurich. Width of relief 119 cm. Cf. pp. 37, 74

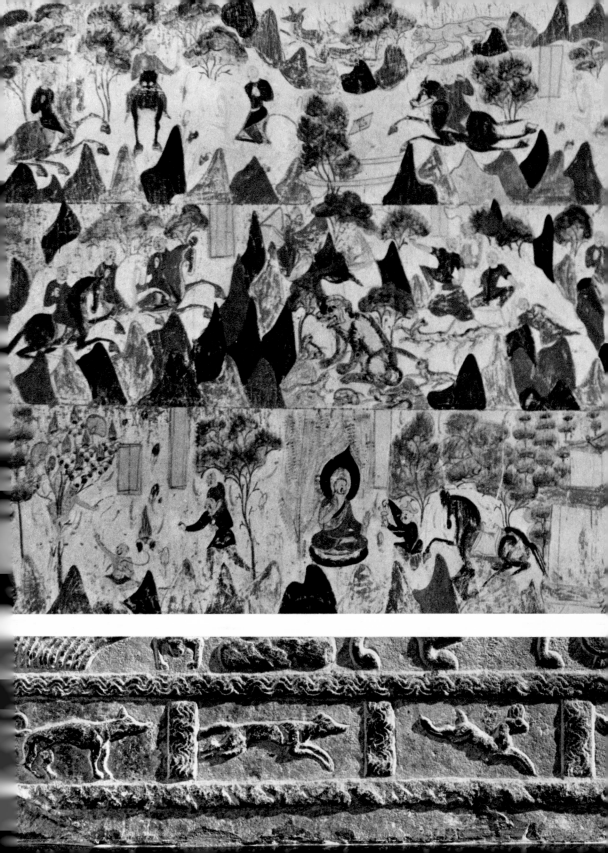

Pages 94, 95 – This large horizontal composition has been identified as one of the stories related in Hsüan Tsang's 'Record of a Journey to the West', *Hsi Yü Chi*, and tells the story of five hundred bandits who ravaged the countryside and, after their defeat by soldiers sent out to subdue them, were punished by having their eyes gouged out. Their cries of agony were heard by the Buddha who was nearby, and overcome by compassion, he caused a cool breeze to blow which relieved their suffering. Later they came to him to hear the message of the Good Law and were converted.

The figure of the queen in the pavilion is explained by Arthur Waley who suggests that she is Mallikā, wife of King Prasenajit, under whose influence the king gave up his cruel ways and became a Buddhist. It was known that on another occasion, when the king intended to kill his cook because he had no dinner ready for him when he turned up unexpectedly, Mallikā intervened on his behalf.

This rendering shows a definite development from our previous plates and we see the beginning of new elements. The narrow registers have been omitted and the 'space cells' are now broken up, giving way to an elegant world of wider horizons, which however still retains the wild exuberance of the lacquer designs with their mythical creatures and floating, swirling, flying figures. The battle scene on the left is animated but rather clumsy, while the scene to the right is more carefully organized with pavilions and a dwelling surrounded by a fenced-in court. This fresco, using elements of previous styles, bursts forth with an entirely new feeling for panoramic landscape. The technique may still be archaic, but, as continually happens in the history of art, a new vision takes what is still useful from the past, and combines it with its own contribution, and creates a vital impulse that is carried on into the centuries that follow.

CAVE 428

Page 96: This shows the right-hand wall of the cave, opposite the Mahāsattva panel. It illustrates the *Viśvantara Jātaka*.

Prince Viśvantara is so generous that one day he even gives away the auspicious white elephant, the harbinger of rain, to a neighbouring kingdom suffering from drought. The angry people demand his banishment, and he leaves for the forest with his wife and two children. During the course of the journey he gives away everything he possesses, including even his two children, to a Brahmin who demands them from him. Eventually even his wife is given away as a servant. In the end, however, Viśvantara gets back his family and returns to his kingdom. This *Jātaka* is very popular in all Buddhist art from India to South-east Asia, Central Asia and China.

CAVE 285: Detail of the plate on pp. 94–95. *Cf. p. 97*

CAVE 285 (A.D. 538–539)

The upper plate on p. 98 is a detail from the ceiling frieze where monks sit in meditation inside huts amidst a landscape of mountains, trees, a lotus pond and bounding deer.

The lower plate on p. 98 depicts a decorative landscape of mountains above the entrance to the cave. This painting is remarkable for its treatment of the mountains, which are executed in bands of stratified blues and greens. As a whole style of green and blue landscape painting developed during the Sui and T'ang dynasties, it is fascinating to observe the invariable use of the green and blue combination in the Wei period. It is used frequently for decorative purposes, as in the concentric circles of colour on early haloes, in the cloud and flame motifs of nimbuses etc., both at Tun-huang and at the Mai-chi Shan caves in Kansu. This floral motif (Fig. 29) from a Han stone rubbing in the Sian Museum is the origin of the floral design used in the Wei period for lintels and borders, both at Tun-huang and at Mai-chi Shan; it is nearly always done in blue and green.
The use of blue and green is so frequent that it is almost a characteristic of the Wei style, and an important decorative factor.
In Wei painting the landscape was still subordinate to the human figure. The mountains were only depicted symbolically, but symbols were just as familiar to the Chinese of that period as they were to medieval Europeans.

Just as in early Buddhist art the figure of the Buddha transcends in size and importance all other figures, so in these paintings the human figures are taller than all other subject-matter, whether mountains or trees, regardless of their proximity. This 'hierarchical perspective' is a natural expression of the minds of men who have not yet fully realized their own place in the universe. This form of thought perspective is common in medieval European art; as late as the sixteenth century El Greco justified the size of figures in a painting as 'celestial beings, which for us are like lights seen from afar that appear large even though they are actually small.'

The only limitations on early landscapes are those of technique and compositional organization. The conception, as nature itself, is already boundless, and the panorama scenes are filled with mountain ranges, lotus ponds and groves of willows, poplars and bamboos. Here we do not find anything similar to the small confined areas of Persian paradise gardens. Nor is nature hostile: there are no dark foreboding forests on the outskirts such as are found until very late in European painting. Saints and sages seek nature and are united with it. Man begins to identify himself with nature, endowing it with significance as a means to achieve spiritual development.

CAVE 299 (early 6th century). Page 101

The upper plate on p. 101 is one of the most interesting in this series. The top panel in the right-hand corner shows a standing figure apparently in a *dhoti*, two figures kneeling before him and two others standing on either side. The central personage is surrounded, from above and on both sides, by long-necked dragons. These dragons are similar in form to those which decorate the cover of an incrusted metal box from pre-Han times (Plate p. 102). Further to the left, riding through the clouds, are the same dragons, accompanied by flying figures and another dragon; the latter also has his counterpart in a Han relief (Fig. 2). This 'celestial' group halts before the summit of a hill where a lion crouches among the rocks in front of a bamboo grove; confronting this scene on the left is a group of 'earthly' figures holding back their rearing horses, preventing them from springing across the intervening space. The horses are drawn with a fine vigorous line, and the lower plate on p. 101 shows them in detail. Light washes of colour give the effect of volume, and the underpart of their bodies has a double line, like that in the Han relief.

The two last registers depict an important, possibly imperial, personage standing and sitting with his retinue at the entrance to the pavilions. This figure has all the solemn dignity of Yen Li-pên's famous portraits of the emperors, though it lacks individualization. The figure in the *dhoti* appears again in the middle register at the extreme left, greeted with reverence by important people.

The diagonals here, made by the roofs of the pavilions, are used rather arbitrarily and are practically the only means used to depict depth, though the rounded mountain summit with rocks before it and the bamboo grove behind in the top register is fairly successful in this respect.

The action is not limited to the fixed viewpoint of a single individual; it goes beyond the individual and becomes a kind of universal conception. The illusion of space is created without harshness. To those familiar with modern art this discretion and lack of emphasis on depth by the Chinese artist will be understandable, for many contemporary European artists are aware that they are unable to solve all their problems through scientific perspective.

'Art which decorates surfaces observes, more or less at all stages of development, a discrete reserve as regards the phenomenon of

Page 102: Tripod with lid. Particularly interesting are the long-necked dragons on the lid. Compare with dragons in the plate on page 88. From finds at Chin-ts'un near Lo-yang (c. 300 B.C.). Bronze inlaid with silver. *Minneapolis Institute of Arts. Height (with lid closed) 15.3 cm. Cf. p. 100*

FIG. 29 – *Rubbing from a stone relief with flower motif. Han dynasty. Sian Museum. Cf. p. 99*

perspective ... depth of space conquered and secured no longer
calls forth enthusiasm as a newly discovered land of wonders.'[8]
The wall space in a Chinese fresco is divided into three planes:
foreground, middle distance, and background; this is known as
san-tieh-fa, 'the law of three sections'.[9] The horizon is not decisive,
and the idea is to convey the impression of infinite space, the eye
wandering from one plane to another.

We may classify the four types of perspective as follows:
yüan-chin: the far and the near, has three divisions and is applied
particularly to landscapes;
shen-yüan: deep distance as seen from below;
kao-yüan: high distance as seen from a height (Fig. 26); and
p'ing-yüan: level distance looking from an object near the foreground
into space.

> In the distance men have no eyes,
> Trees have no branches, mountains
> No stones and water no waves.'
> *Wang Wei*
> (8th century)

[8] M. J. Friedländer, *On Art and Connoisseurship*, London, 1942, pp. 66, 68.
[9] B. March, op. cit., paras. 161–4.

IV. THE SUI DYNASTY (A.D. 589–618)

I shall play on my *ch'in* the air of the restless pine forests.
Raising my cup I shall ask the Moon to join me.
The Moon and the Wind will always be my friends.
My fellow creatures here below are but transitory companions.[1]

Li Po
(A.D. 701–752)

After two hundred and seventy-one years China was again united under the Sui dynasty. Their empire extended from the southernmost point of Fukien province and Annam to the Great Wall in the north-west.

The Sui emperor Yang-ti was brilliant, temperamental and unstable. He was a most ardent patron of art and literature, and advocated 'that those who have gained renown for themselves by their war-like energy return to a study of the Classics.'

He planned and constructed part of the canal which united north and south China up to modern times. This enterprise is reputed to have been inspired by a landscape painting hanging in his palace. For this 'roads were constructed along both banks and planted with elms and willows. For over two thousand *li* from Lo-yang to Hang-chow shadows of trees overlapped each other.' Three million six hundred thousand labourers worked on the canal and with those who helped to supply them the number was brought to 5,430,000. The canal system assured communication and the transport of food from China's greatest source, the lower reaches of the Yangtze. Other immense construction schemes were undertaken without regard to cost in money or lives. Yang-ti was extravagant, and not being content with one capital at Ch'ang-an (Sian), he built a

[1] R. Grousset, *The Rise and Splendour of the Chinese Empire*, tr. A. Watson-Gandy and T. Gordon, London, 1952, p. 153.

second at Lo-yang and a third at Hang-chow on the lower Yangtze. There are endless descriptions of Yang-ti's love of festivals and fêtes on the lake at Lo-yang, and of the opening of the great water-way when 'hundreds of many-tiered barges took the entire court down the canal.' Pomp and luxury were Yang-ti's downfall and it is said of him that 'he shortened the life of his dynasty by a number of years but benefited posterity into ten thousand generations.'

With the short-lived Sui dynasty a transitional period began, during which the arts, in the stability engendered by the newly-found unity, burst into flower.

The elements which form the character of this transition are, like those of all periods of development, full of fascination. Old motifs are transformed and new ones appear. It is this continual com-bination of the old and the new which makes the Sui frescoes at Tun-huang among the most entrancing and the most difficult to understand. They are finer and more elegant than those of the Wei; personages become more realistic and their movement clearer. There is a search for improved organization; the use of architecture predominates, and the roofs and walls take on the same importance as did the old saw-toothed hills under the Wei in delineating space and giving movement and depth. Light wooden structures with doors, curtains and windows separate one scene from another, while half-open windows and doors, diagonally placed roofs, walls, balustrades and stairs are used with great effect to give the illusion of depth.

These light pavilions with people inside and outside them, sitting and standing, are another constant feature in Chinese art. We saw this used in the bronze basin of the Warring States period (Fig. 13) and Figure 30 is taken from a painting on lacquer ware of the same era.

FIGS. 13, 30

In the Sui frescoes at Tun-huang the hills are still present, but

FIG. 30 – *Lacquer from Changsha. Warring States period*

unlike the previous period it is as if the artist does not know where to put them now that his world has been invaded by architecture and trees. He has lost interest in those old saw-toothed hills and uses them merely as dark accents in his composition of lines and feathery brush-strokes.

If animals were popular at the court with such painters as Yen Li-pên and others, they were no less so at Tun-huang. Horses are superbly conceived; we see them in procession, galloping in the hunt, and drinking calmly from a trough; they have the same long narrow heads and slender legs as in the Wei stone reliefs.

Some of the animals are executed in the *po-hua*, or plain drawing PLATE P. 108 technique; Dr Waley in his *Introduction to the Study of Chinese Painting* says that red and black lines formed the outlines, which were filled in with light washes of colour to indicate volume and emphasize contours. He says that in the fourth century this technique was used in the painting of a hunting scene in the Upper Park at Ch'ang-an, and that later Wu Tao-tzŭ excelled in *po-hua*. The other technique used for animals bears witness to the early use of *mo-ku* or 'boneless painting' – that is, only washes of colour without any outlines at all. Line here has all the excitement of a living, vital element, and is the main factor here, as it always is in Chinese art. This is a calligraphic quality, and is even extended to the architecture, which is meant to be seen as a façade (J. Buhot); in Indian art, for example, it is the sculptural quality that dominates, even in architecture which is conceived in the round.

In these frescoes the drawing is often done in red chalk and then gone over with a very fine black or red brush-stroke. If we compare the lines in the Han mural from Hopei, we see that a broad line PLATES PP. 58, 59 BELOW is used to emphasize the upper part of the bodies of animals; but in the stone reliefs this line is used for the neck and chest, which is the technique used here in the rendering of horses. There are many indications that the artists were both sculptors and painters and that they often transferred the technique of the brush to work PLATE P. III BELOW in stone or from stone or metal to the brush. This is also true of the treatment of the trees and stratified mountains.

In Sui art it appears as if one of the rules laid down for landscapes

CAVE 296 (*c.* A.D. 600). Pages 110, 111

A two-registered composition shows a caravan of camels and horses entering and leaving a fortified enclosure. At the top left are groups of nobles standing outside the walls, under trees amid rocks. The vertical lines of the trees and the fur trimming on the robes contrast with the circular forms of the baggage borne by the animals; the diagonal movement of the roofs adds a third rhythm. Again *po-hua* is used for the animals, with the double line for the lower part of the horses, as in the Han relief (Fig. 2). The camel caravan, richly embellished and colourful, is particularly impressive. *Cf. p. 107*

seems to have been taken literally: 'the important tree or trees are the first thing to be sketched; then the landscape or the terrain is built around them' (Chieh Tzǔ Yüan Hua Chuan). For in many of these plates the trees are a background screen for the action taking place in the foreground. The treatment of trees is sheer enchantment for the eye. Never have they been so tenderly observed or rendered with such delicate verve. We find trees of every conceivable variety painted in as many different ways. In the plate on page 118–9 the willow is handled in an impressionistic manner with

FIG. 31 – *Rubbing from an engraved stone sarcophagus, c. A.D. 525 Nelson Gallery of Art, Kansas City. Cf. p. 116*

CAVE 296 (*c.* A.D. 600)

The two scenes on p. 111 are details taken from a horizontal panel which permit closer observation of the effortless brushwork. In the lower plate on the right a group of nobles are standing under trees, while a cavalier accompanied by standard-bearers rides through a rocky landscape. His horse is drawn with a soft broad brush-stroke emphasizing the neck and chest, while his attendant's horses have the entire lower part of their bodies done in a dark colour wash.

The wall-painting below is not done in the same technique as the frescoes on pages 101 above, 108, 111. Here line is almost entirely absent and the brush is used with washes of colour on broad surfaces. The effect of light and air is produced with fine sensitivity, with the trees and leaves often conveyed impressionistically by gentle dabs of the brush; they form a continuous screen and a soft canopy above the hard forms of the rocks below. They accentuate the composition vertically; depth is suggested by the zigzag lines of the roofs and the oblique placing of the balustrades and curtained doors.

Page 112: CAVE 302 (early 6th century)
Caption on pp. 118–9

Plate on p. 113, CAVE 301 (early 7th century). These two plates are examples of a technique combining light touches of the brush with the coiled curves of the old cloud-scroll mountain. The movement is rampant and impetuous, as if the artist had lost control of his brush and, possessed by a demon, was driven into this paroxysm of furious energy. The flying figures in the plate on p. 113, seen in the sky on either side of the pagoda, have now developed into arabesques galloping on banks of clouds as light as thistledown. The colonettes of the pagoda have curtains looped over their capitals; this characteristic of the Wei shrine is often seen at Tun-huang and sometimes at Mai-chi Shan. In the plate on p. 113 we notice that the willow-tree is treated in a different manner from those in the previous plates.

Page 114 above: CAVE 420 (c. A.D. 600). Lotus ponds full of birds and encircled by saw-toothed hills and trees are seen above the flame-decorated nimbus of the central Buddha. Directly above is a scene with the attendants Vimalakīrti and Mañjuśrī and a great concourse of people. Here the pavilions holding Vimalakīrti and Mañjuśrī are quite separate from the lotus ponds, but it is interesting to note that the elaborate palace structures in later paradise scenes have supports rising directly out of the lotus ponds. It would be extremely useful to study the way in which these majestic Wei group compositions within an architectural frame developed into the T'ang paradise scenes which dominate most of the two hundred T'ang caves at Tun-huang. The later paradise scenes have landscape panels on either side. *Cf. p. 173*

Page 114 below: CAVE 419 (A.D. 589–618)
Further plates on pp. 123, 124. Caption on p. 122

sweeping washes of colour, at the extreme right-hand corner in quite another manner, delicately and minutely, and at the top left in a third style. Comparison of the treatment of the trees with those in stone reliefs of the same period is enlightening. The plume-like trees swaying in the wind have their exact counterpart in the FIG. 31 sarcophagus reliefs dated A.D. 525, in the Nelson Gallery of Art, Kansas City. In fact there are many elements in this relief similar to those found in these murals. They are both narrow horizontal compositions; the figures are still large in relation to landscape; and the hills, animals and trees give the continuity necessary to an illustrative or narrative composition, with the repetition of the same characters in successive scenes. While in the murals the diagonals are achieved almost entirely through architecture, in the sarcophagus the forms of the mountains are often used to obtain the same effect, for they have straight horizontal lines on the top, as if they were plateaux.

However, in most of the Tun-huang plates in question the sense of PLATES PP. 118-9 depth is not as developed as it is in the reliefs, though our plate is perhaps ahead in this respect, particularly in the upper register, for there is a great advance in the relative importance of the figures to the landscape; as Dr Soper points out, in Sui art the background, 'the near and the far', is developed while the middle distance is usually neglected. However, in this plate the figures are well integrated into the landscape.

As trees assume an importance in this period, and also in landscape generally, it is interesting that among the ways of painting them three were of importance: *han-lin*, or cold forest trees without leaves; *ch'iao-chih*, with branches like birds' claws, usually suggested by three or more vertical strokes together; *huo-yen chih*, with branches resembling flames, indicated by curving sweeping strokes. Different techniques were employed for the leaves, mainly with the use of *tien* (dots) of various kinds: small, light and dark, even-headed, curved, upswept, drooping, sharply pointed; their use varied according to the importance of the trees in the composition, the distance, or the artist's desire to convey a special impression, such as that of leaves in midsummer heavy with rain, a distant forest etc.

CAVE 302 (early 7th century). Pages 112, 118–9

A Bodhisattva, top right, sits on a lotus throne under a willow-tree and beside him stands a figure wearing a short *dhoti* and a scarf that hangs down, the upper part of his body bare; light wooden houses with half-open doors and windows suggest depth. The whole painting is done with colour washes, the only lines are those of branches of trees, the pillars and woodwork of the pavilions, which are done in a brush line. The attitude of the figures is lively, and the gestures of the hands and heads are very expressive.

CAVE 299 (late 6th or early 7th century)

This is one of the most beautiful hunting landscape scenes at Tun-huang. The bowman on the left shooting at a bounding deer is evidently a personage of importance, as an attendant is holding a

parasol above him. The treatment of the willow-tree, on the extreme right, is most interesting, for it differs from that of earlier times. It is executed in a light wash of colour with *tien* (dots) for the leaves. All these murals have, as is usual at Tun-huang, a frieze of flying figures.

CAVE 419 (A.D. 589–618). Plates pp. 114 below, 123 above and 124

The panels shown in the lower plate on p. 114 and on p. 123 are quite different in character from those in the previous plates; they are painted in deep sombre colours, black and strong blue, with green and white relieving the dark tones. At the top of the lower plate on p. 114 there is a ceiling panel, here shown upside down. The dark blue roofs begin to invade the composition, which still has three registers although this division is here beginning to break down. The lower plate on p. 114 may show the Prince Sudhāna Jātaka; the upper plate on p. 123 is a detail of the middle register.

CAVE 420 (c. A.D. 600). Plates pp. 114 above and 123 below

A ceiling panel from Cave 420. This complex scene of temples and pagodas with zigzag walls is one of the most curious compositions to be found at Tun-huang. The pale blue walls and roofs of the plate on pp. 128–9 are here a dark intense blue which dominates the whole picture, creating a heavy rhythm. The hills are now definitely banished to small 'space cells' in the background. The movement is broken in the centre by a decorated chariot accompanied by nobles; the procession ends in the lower foreground where two Buddhas are seated on lotus thrones, surrounded by an assembly of persons. The Buddha on the left has over him a canopy and a tree of the same type that is painted on the silk scrolls from Tun-huang in the British Museum. Figures stand, kneel or sit around the central characters in the temples; in the middle right a Buddha is preaching to an audience; and in the extreme left of the foreground a man is being attacked by wolves.

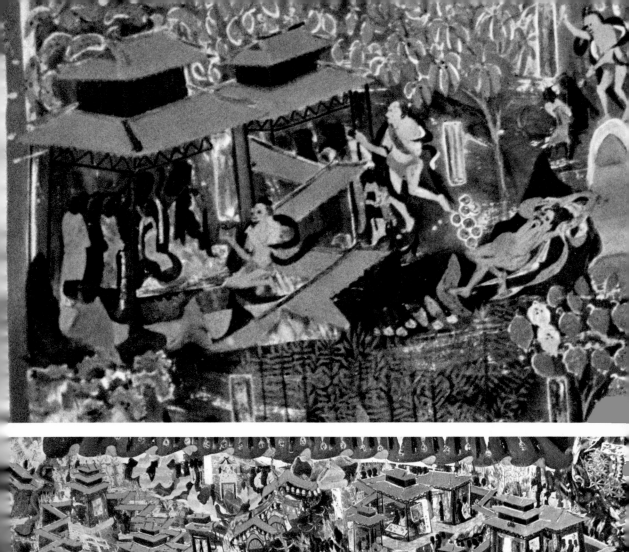

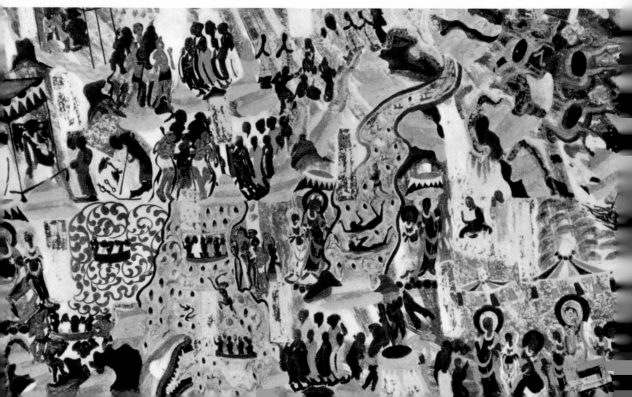

CAVE 419 (A.D. 585–617)

Two ceiling panels (p. 124). The upper plate is divided by a central sacred mountain with a bamboo grove on its right and pine-trees below its summit. For the first time we see an attempt at a massive peak, which dominates the centre of the composition; the shading to indicate the contours is very crudely executed. At the top on the right-hand side are two seated Buddhas, probably Śākyamuni and Prabūtaratna, under a canopy. Their two attendants are wearing the draped scarves common to the Late Sui and Early T'ang Bodhisattvas. To the left, above a pond with mandarin ducks, fish and lotus blossoms, stand two figures on lotus pedestals surrounded by a large group of persons, kneeling or standing. Above a man appears to be leaping into the fire, while a monk with folded hands looks on. In contrast to the crude technique of shading on the mountain, the bamboo grove is delicately painted in every detail; knots on the stems are minutely indicated. The artist was apparently on familiar ground. The right-hand side of this painting may depict the *Lotus Sūtra*, and that on the left the *Fa-hua Sūtra*, where a man leaps into the fire while virtuous people stand by worshipping Kuan-yin (Avalokiteśvara), and are happy and safe. *Cf. pp. 114 below and 123 above.*

CAVE 303 (early 7th century)

In most caves the bottom register of the walls is reserved for portraits of donors. This detail shows a carriage with a noblewoman inside, drawn by an ox. The charioteer is standing by the animal while behind the carriage, on foot, are four female attendants wearing long high-waisted robes of Sui ladies. They are journeying through a sandy desert landscape, the undulations being indicated by faint brush-strokes. The carriage is very much like those used today in the region of Tun-huang. For the ox only a light wash of colour is used, without line. *Cf. p. 17*

126

There were special brush-strokes for the leaves of specific trees, the most common of which were pine, cedar, plum, willow, *wu-t'ung* (sterculia phatamfolia) also called the phoenix tree, firs, the Tree of Heaven (silanthus surna), small willows, young bamboos; there was even a special *tien* for pine-needles. Our figures show various methods of depicting trees from pre-Han times onwards; this FIGS. 32 A–L selection makes no claim to be complete.

This composition, although it starts as usual from the right, appears to have three different beginnings, at the points where groups of people move from the right towards the pavilions or temples on the left. From top left a diagonal movement of rocks and hills cuts across the painting to a waterfall, which itself continues down towards the extreme right of the foreground. This oblique motion from left to right contrasts with the upward movement from right to left of recurring figures of men and women carrying children on their shoulders. Each pavilion is placed in a circular unit of rocks. The lower range of rocky hills is heavier and denser than the others; in the middle foreground a river runs through a rocky gorge. Some of the figures are partly hidden by walls, with only their heads appearing to suggest depth. The absence of trees is notable and those that do exist are indicated very casually. Pale blue roofs add a zigzag movement within each spatial unit. The colouring is light and gives an impression of elegance.

FIG. 32 – *Various ways of depicting trees. Cf. p. 127*

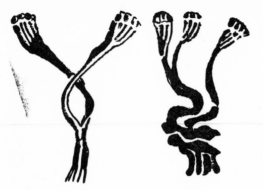 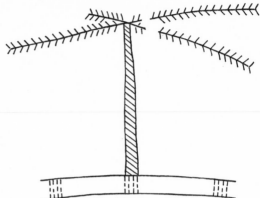

A. *Bronze mirror, pre-Han. Freer Gallery of Art, Washington*

B. *Bronze basin. Warring States period. Archaeological Museum, Peking*

 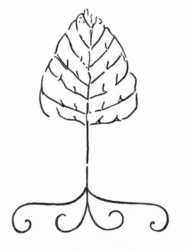 

C. *Lacquer painting from Changsha, pre-Han*

D. *Tile, pre-Han*

E. *Bronze mirror, pre-Han. Freer Gallery of Art, Washington*

F. *Wu-t'ung: tree with branches pointing upwards*

G. *Fu-sang: tree with sun-bird*

H. *Wu-t'ung: tree in blossom with branches hanging down*

I. *After a Sui fresco from Tun-huang*

K. *After a stone relief on a sarcophagus, dated A.D. 525 Nelson Gallery of Art, Kansas City*

L. *After a stone relief on a sarcophagus, dated A.D. 525 Nelson Gallery of Art, Kansas City*

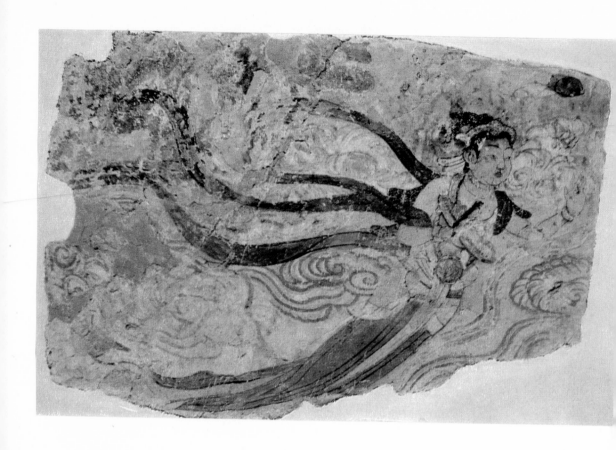

Apsaras strewing flowers flying from left to right against a background of clouds. The representation of wind-swept garments is typical of T'ang painting. This fragment once occupied a place in Kinnari cave at Kumtura (Kuchā – Kyzyl area), on the upper left-hand part of the rear wall, beside the niche containing Buddha's image. 8th–9th centuries A.D. *Dept. of Indian Art, Ehem. Staatliche Museen, Berlin. 58 × 39 cm. Cf. p. 47*

V. THE T'ANG DYNASTY (A.D. 618–906)

> In limpid autumn nothing obscures my view;
> On the horizon a light mist is rising.
> A distant river melts into the sky,
> And a solitary city sinks in the milky mist.
> A few last leaves are falling,
> blown by the breeze;
> The sun sets behind the curving hills.
> How late the solitary crane returns!
> In the twilight the rooks are
> already flocking to the forest.[1]
>
> *Tu Fu*
> (A.D. 712–770)

The T'ang rulers held China together for three hundred years, continuing the unity brought about by the Sui emperors. Their rule extended as far as the Pamirs and Kashmir in the west and from the Yellow Sea to Annam in the south. In the seventh and eighth centuries Ch'ang-an 'was the capital of the world as Rome was in the Middle Ages and Paris later.'[2]

Her streets, cosmopolitan and international, were thronged with foreign traders and envoys, monks from India, artists from Central Asia, students from Korea and Japan, merchants from Persia, Arabs and Turks; Zoroastrians, Manicheans and Nestorian Christians mixed with Buddhists, Taoists and Muslims. They built their temples and worshipped, each according to their fashion. It was the same in the south China ports. In Canton alone there were over 120,000 foreigners. In Ch'ang-an, Hang-chow, Ch'üan-chou and Canton quarters of the cities were set aside for them. Among the foreigners was an artist monk from 'the country of the Lion (Ceylon)', who we are told 'painted figures of the Buddha in a grave and dignified manner.'

[1] R. Grousset, op. cit., p. 155.
[2] A. Waley, op. cit., p. 97.

All Asia sent its goods to Ch'ang-an; an increasing number of camel caravans carried silk, tea, camphor and aloes to the Middle East, while ships sailed with cargoes bound for India, and eventually Tarsus, Jerusalem and Alexandria. Chinese nobles got their horses from Ferghana, their falcons from the Uighurs and Tokharians, while ladies dressed *à l'occidentale* in the Persian fashion attended the royal garden-parties and strolled by the lakes and canals.

'Beside the waters of Ch'ang-an are many lovely women with graceful step and distant air,' sang Tu Fu. 'Their garments of embroidered silk reflect the light of spring, the gold-embrocaded peacock and the silver unicorn. What are the ladies wearing on their heads? Iridescent feathers – flowers that hang before their ears, sashes sewn with pearls closely fit their waists.'

The Emperor Hsüan-tsung's reign (712–756) was the most brilliant; his name is inseparable from the tragic and beautiful concubine Yang Kuei-fei, the Flying Swallow of Li Po's poem.

> Who is the most beautiful?
> It is the flying swallow who
> makes her nest in the palace.
> The clouds are like her dress
> The flowers her face . . .[3]

She was however the cause of one of the most destructive rebellions which virtually ended this reign, and was killed by the emperor's guards in front of him. 'Her flower-worked clasp fell to the ground and nobody picked it up. Her kingfisher pin and her comb of purest jade; the sovereign covered his eyes but could not save her life. His tears mingled with her blood' (Po Chü-i).

Hsüan-tsung never recovered from this and abandoned the throne to his son, for he longed eternally for her 'flower face and black cloud temples; their short spring nights passed within perfumed curtains.' Yang Kuei-fei's unusual type (she was plump) inspired the new T'ang beauty reflected in the paintings, such as we see at Tun-huang.

This was China's great age of poetry: 'whoever was a man was a

PLATES PP. 158,
162–3

[3] R. Grousset, op. cit., p. 156.

poet.' The famous names were Li Po, Tu Fu, Po Chü-i and the landscapist Wang Wei. Po Chü-i was probably the first poet ever to have his poems printed, in A.D. 800–810; he was popular in Korea and Japan, where he was made the hero of a Nō play. Religious poetry was produced in abundance and there was a growing demand for thousands of books; editions of linguistic and historical works appeared and by the ninth century a printed book was accepted as quite normal both inside and outside China.

We may use the example of literature in our approach to painting. Chinese poetry reached its apogee during the T'ang, and reveals a vitality which is closely inspired by popular forms. The Sung period was a continuation of the T'ang and became more refined and polished, and perhaps, in spite of its beauty, rather precious; it inevitably lost strength and vigour, which is what distinguishes the T'ang from the Sung. In the Yüan period, following the Sung, new forms in literature appear, the novel and the opera, but poetry never reached the heights of the T'ang epoch.

Many Chinese critics have divided the painting of this epoch into northern and southern schools, to correspond to the separation between the northern and southern school of Ch'an Buddhism which also took place at this time. However, this theory is no longer considered tenable.

It appears that the artist Li Ssŭ-hsün and his son Li Chao-tao originated one style of painting and Wang Wei the landscapist another style; his paintings, we are told, were saturated with poetic under-currents. Tung-p'o, describing the work of Wang Wei and Wu Tao-tzŭ, says that Wang Wei was born a poet and 'carried the fragrant iris at his waist; he had the wings of an immortal to soar above the cage; whoever reads Wang's poems finds pictures in them and whoever looks at his pictures finds poems in them.' And on Wu Tao-tzŭ he says: 'Wu was indeed bold and free, grand as the rolling waves of the sea; his hand moved as swiftly as the wind and the rain, there was life even in the places where his brush did not reach.'

Around these names – the two Li, Wang Wei and Wu Tao-tzŭ – there has accumulated a great deal of literature, and many anecdotes

CAVE 103 (A.D. 713–762). Plates pp. 137, 142

This is a vertical narrative landscape. The white elephant carries sacred texts on its back and shows Hsüan Tsang on his way from India to China. It is accompanied by a monk on a horse, a mahout or elephant-driver who is walking in front, and two attendants. Arthur Waley has remarked that on Hsüan Tsang's return from India in 643–644 the Indian king Harsha of Kanauj gave him a truly royal gift of a white elephant. The elephant unfortunately drowned near Kashgar. This scene must therefore represent the return journey after Hsüan Tsang had received the gift. In the middle distance on the right are the tall towers of three city-gates flanked by trees. The travellers proceed through a plain surrounded by ranges of mountains and after a hazardous journey emerge out of a narrow mountain pass in the middle foreground; the monk dismounts at the side of a waterfall by a pool and clasps his hands in thanksgiving for the safe journey. Short pines cling to the mountain ridges; creepers and ferns festoon the slopes; bamboo grass grows on the elevation in the left foreground. *Kou-le* is used to outline the contours of the mountains and line for the elephant, the horse and the figures. Washes of colour indicate volume.

CAVE 321 (A.D. 618–712 and 907–959)

This is a detail of a landscape showing a mountainous stretch of country, treated with light washes of graded colour; the two elephants and two horses in the centre are painted differently from the animals in the plate on p. 137. Washes of colour are the main element; white lines are used as outlines, and also as high-lights on the high mountain peaks in the foreground (below, right) and on the elephants. A bird and a dark-skinned figure in a *dhoti* appear at the top on the right; on the left in the middle are standing two men, one with a lion mask. These figures must represent hour spirits, for each hour had its animal spirit, after which it was named: e.g., Hour of the Boar, Hour of the Tiger, etc.

are told of them, particularly of the great Wu. They were all at the court of the emperor Hsüan, and with the poets formed the 'nine jewels' of this brilliant reign.

Li Ssŭ-hsün (*c.* 650–716) and his son Li Chao-tao used brilliant colours for their landscapes, the *Ch'ing-pi shan-shui*, or mainly blue and green, and the *Ch'ing-lu shan-shui*, or outlined with gold. They made use of architecture, palaces, open galleries, 'lofty terraces, pavilions, vast stretches of imaginative landscape, mountain peaks piercing the clouds, streams spanned by arched bridges ... the whole in a transparent veil of poetic vision' (Sirén). As we noticed in Chapters III and IV both the use of blue and green and architectural elements come from Wei and Han times. It is here brought to a matchless apogee of decorative fantasy in landscape painting and started a style that continued for a thousand years.

Wang Wei (699–759) was a devout Buddhist and a follower of Wei-mo-ch'i the sage (Vimalakīrti). Wang Wei's style name was Mo-ch'i after his preceptor. During the rebellion Wang Wei was forced to serve the rebel chief and was saved later because of a poem he wrote, 'The Frozen Pearl', which moved the emperor to forgive him. He retired and lived in seclusion in his country house Wang-ch'üan; one of his most famous paintings is a horizontal scroll of the landscape around his home. Several copies of this work still exist, and it would be interesting to compare one with certain

PLATE P. 141   conventions of composition and perspective in our plates. The copy in the British Museum and a rubbing done from a stone relief after Wang Wei's painting show us the same horizontal composition, with a winding river as a unifying element, and though there is perfection and maturity in the conception, it is still in a sense the

Page 141: Wang-ch'üan, the country house of the well-known T'ang poet Wang Wei (699–759). This painting is presumably by his own hand. Today only copies survive of this horizontal scroll; the detail shown here is from a copy in the British Museum. *Cf. above*

old spatial unit made up of hills and mountains. The mountains themselves have changed but the idea of the spatial unit forming a framework for the subject still remains. And in this connection one can agree entirely with the critic Chang Yen-yüan who said 'Wang Wei painted landscapes in a style which connected the old with the modern.'

This phenomenon of an ancient form of composition persisting over centuries until it is brought to perfection and maturity is also seen in Indian art, when the early stone medallions of the Buddhist stūpas, from the third century B.C., caused the scenes to be composed in circular form. This early primitive form goes on until, in the Ajantā frescoes of the sixth and seventh centuries, it reaches such perfection that at first one is not conscious that the scene is in fact a circular composition (Auboyer).

Wu Tao-tzǔ held an official post at court and was a friend of Prince Ning, the emperor's brother. There has been so much written about him that we need not go into great detail about his work or life. One story, however, is particularly relevant to us. The emperor, we are told, sent Wu and Li to make pictures of the Shu country. Li came back with careful sketches and later painted 'rushing waters, winding streams, vaporous effects of rosy clouds at sunset reminding us of the abodes of the immortals.'

Wu brought nothing back and when the emperor asked to see his studies he bowed and said 'Your servant has made no sketches, they are all in his heart.' And when he took up the brush in inspiration he completed the most magnificent painting, embracing hundreds of miles of rivers and mountains.

The overwhelming impression of T'ang painting at Tun-huang is

Page 142: CAVE 103 (A.D. 713–762): caption on p. 136

CAVE 323 (A.D. 618–712 and 960–1278). Plates pp. 3, 151

This cave is probably one of the most beautiful T'ang caves at Tun-huang. The painting has a superb quality and is by the hand of a great master. The Sung additions are mainly in the short corridor leading into the cave.

The upper plate on p. 151 shows a boat with a typical Chinese hull and broad stern and bow, rowed by two boatmen; two other monks and a lay figure surround two great statues of the standing Buddha. This is thought to show the arrival in Canton of the famous sandalwood statue sent by an Indian king to a Chinese emperor of the Liang dynasty in the sixth century. Various figures are shown welcoming it, kneeling in worship. Among these figures are monks wearing robes with a familiar large check pattern typical of T'ang Lohans (disciples). The inscription on the tablet to the left reads, in rough translation: 'Whenever faith exists it will not be altered by human affairs. Those

CAVE 323

who believe deeply in the Buddha consider it possible that when the Buddha arrives the wind and the waves will remain quiet. Thereby he will be welcome to the temple T'ung-hsuan-ssu and be worshipped for ever.'

The plate on p. 144 is a detail of the plate on p. 151 above; a man carrying a lotus is riding on an ox with a child beside him, accompanied by two other persons; the woman behind him also carries a lotus flower; they seem to be hurrying so as not to be late for the great event.

Although the landscape itself is done in the *mo-ku* method, the folds of the robes, especially those of the Buddhas, are executed by white lines. The figures are in the same style as those in the plates on pages 158, 162–3 and are vividly expressive: even the backs of the two monks who are kneeling before the boat tell us something. Foreshortening of the figures is here used to great effect.

The line of the bank runs diagonally from the middle of the background to the left, accentuated by the figures along the shore. The boat and the figures run in an oblique line to this. The right side of the picture is taken up by vertical lines and volumes depicting hills, the posts of the palanquin, the tablets and, finally, the two strong static figures of the statues, which almost form an apex and give the whole an irregular triangle effect.

The lower plate on p. 151 portrays Chang Ch'ien, the first Chinese ambassador to Central Asia, sent by the Han emperor Wu Ti in the middle of the second century B.C. (see chapter 1), as he crosses the desert riding on a piebald horse, with his retinue walking beside and behind him. An attendant is holding a decorated parasol over him. These are highly accentuated outlines, strongly reminiscent of some Han figures. The inscription reads: 'In the time of (the emperor) Chun Tsung in the Han, they obtained a golden figure but did not recognize the name, so the marquis of Po-Wang, Chan Ch'ien, was sent to the West. This shows the moment when he received this commission from the emperor.'

The plate on p. 145 is a pure landscape scene of rivers and high mountains, showing three men being conveyed across a river in a sailing-boat rowed by two oarsmen. It is distinguished by the light effect mentioned on page 155; it is entirely done in *mo-ku*, with great simplicity and beauty.

The plate on p. 3 (Cave 323) shows a desert with mountains in the background, a seven-storeyed pagoda rising towards the sky, before which six figures are standing in reverence. The pagoda is similar to one of the earliest wooden pagodas at Hōkiji near Nara in Japan, which has a square plan and follows Chinese T'ang design. The composition is a balanced asymmetrical one as was common in Sung paintings, particularly those of Mi Fei. The chief stress is on the left, with rising amber-shaded mountains crowned by distant peaks in black. This line is reinforced by the black vertical form of the pagoda, its structural details rendered by white brush lines. On the right this is balanced by low hills and dark vertical figures, completed by the tablet to the right of the pagoda. The harmony of this composition makes it one of the most satisfactory landscapes in all Chinese art.

146

its strength and powerful vitality. It has been the custom to compare the Tun-huang frescoes with those of the same period in the Hōryūji temple in Japan. Though the effect of the Hōryūji frescoes is perhaps refined, they have nothing like the power of the Tun-huang murals, where the brush-strokes seem charged with a dynamic life of their own.

The Tun-huang Institute authorities in their studies on this epoch divide the 206 T'ang caves into four groups:

Early: A.D. 618–712
Climactic: A.D. 713–765
Middle: A.D. 766–820
Late: A.D. 821–860

However, for the purpose of this book the plates are not grouped by this method.

During the T'ang period subject-matter changes and the Jātaka stories, the favourites of the Wei and Sui periods, are practically never painted. The paradise scene becomes predominant (every T'ang cave has at least two). They are great complex groups of figures in an architectural frame with secular scenes and landscapes in panels on either side. Another favourite subject was the *Fa-hua Sūtra*, which was painted with great gusto. Historical scenes and portraits abound: ambassadors going out into far countries, pilgrims bringing back sacred texts on the backs of elephants and horses; ships with monks and statues on board sailing into harbours; while princesses and emperors with their retinues line the lower half of the walls.

In nearly all these landscapes the technique used has now changed from the earlier period. It has been liberated by the bright sunlight of T'ang rationalism. The conception is unrestricted by division into registers and the remarkable simplicity of treatment shows a deep understanding of the technique needed for mural painting as opposed to painting on silk. These frescoes, although similar in spirit and conception to the T'ang silk landscapes, cannot be compared in actual execution with the silk scrolls, since the brush used for a mural must be quite different.

It is surprising to see here, in the T'ang period, the two techniques

CAVE 209 (A.D. 763–820). Plates pp. 149, 152

The upper plate on p. 152 and on p. 149 show two of the most beautiful landscapes of the T'ang period. Unfortunately the mural in the plate on p. 152 was damaged by some vandal who made a charcoal drawing to the left of it.

The plate on p. 149 shows part of a high mountain range. The composition is built up in successive cones as in some Wei drawing, and is reminiscent of the stamped brick illustrated in Fig. 14. A pool or mountain lake is on the left in the foreground. Two scenes are rendered simultaneously. At the top on the right is a Buddha preaching to a group of women who are wearing the high ornamental head-dress of the Late Sui or Early T'ang periods. It is executed in line and wash while the trees are treated in an 'impressionistic' technique with dabs of colour.

The upper plate on p. 152 is a companion-piece done in the same technique and by the same artist. The composition is slightly different: at the top on the left the line of the mountain continues, leading us further up, while the action takes place on one of the lower slopes. Here a Buddha, assisted by two attendants, is preaching to a group of women; lower down a monk is seen standing at the entrance to a cave cut into the slope.

The lower plate on p. 152 gives a view of the rear wall of the cave with landscapes on either side of the central nimbus. The wall-paintings shown in the upper plate on p. 152 and on p. 149 are to be found on the adjoining lateral walls; we can just see them in this photograph. The scene above the nimbus gives us a very good idea of the exuberance of movement in some of the T'ang caves. The images have been removed and we see the blank space where they were fixed to the wall. *Cf. p. 64*

Page 151 above (CAVE 323):
caption on pp. 144, 145

Page 151 below (CAVE 323):
caption on p. 146

靈應西之不在人事
信佛浮者以為俳
及遠靜經迷
玄字似來迴至于
風及凰宮向

generally associated with Sung painting, when they were thought to have started. The first appears to be a development of the old *po-hua* technique of line and colour wash which we saw used for some of the Sui frescoes. However, here it has gone further, and the fine outlines are combined with varying colour washes as in our plates. This seems to correspond to the first Sung academic PLATES PP. 144, 151 style, where fine contour lines are filled with washes of colour, according to the *kou-le-t'ien-ts'ai* technique or the *kou-le* or contour method.

The other appears to be a technique of using graded colour washes alone, and perhaps corresponds to the second academic style called *mo-ku* or boneless 'line suppressed' style as in our plate, where it is PLATE P. 169 generally (although not exclusively) used for desert landscapes. The touches of white and black against the background colour of dark and pale amber washes are very effective, and as a technique which gives the atmospheric quality of light and space found in those regions it is admirable.

In this simplified form of expression the grandeur of vision and the immense desert landscapes of the 'Sand and Melon' country are truly revealed. The wide empty spaces are full of depth; they are bathed in a light which is that of the mirage; the rhythmic contours of arid mountains melt into the horizon; every object appears to be distinct but in reality, when one tries to obtain a clear view, it seems unreal and elusive, for ever escaping one's vision, like man's eternal dream of liberation and happiness – always before him, never with him.

Man takes his place within the grandeur of nature; he travels through it, busy about his immediate concerns; or we see him

Page 152 above (CAVE 209):
caption on p. 148

Page 152 below (CAVE 209):
caption on p. 148

CAVE 217 (late 7th century). Pages 155, 157, 161

This celebrated landscape in the plate on p. 155 is another example of a vertical narrative landscape composition like that on p. 137. It may possibly represent the voyage of Hsüan Tsang (602–664) to India. We see the straw-hatted figure on a horse (top right) and then journeying through thousands of miles of countryside with deep mountain gorges and plains, stopping on the way for rest and shelter in forts and cities. Below to the left he is shown being received by a royal personage in a typically Chinese architectural structure.

The conception, as in the plate on p. 137, is typically T'ang, executed with soft colour washes and fluid brush-strokes. Though it is no longer divided into registers and is vertical, nevertheless the various stages of the traveller's journey do divide the picture into horizontal zones. The perspective is that of the now familiar 'shifting point of vision', 'the hovering or dynamic view region'. We are able to participate in the action: we cross the mountain pass, we enter the Tibetan-looking fort on the right, and we talk with the princely group in the palace on the left (cf. detail in the plate on p. 161). The vision extends to the distant horizon where the mountain ranges recede among the clouds. A river rising in the range furthest to the left meanders down diagonally, sometimes hidden by the hill in the plain, until it cascades over the steep cliffs in the right of the foreground.

When our pilgrim reaches the country shown in the centre it is spring, for trees in blossom line the river-bank and the slopes of the hills. Ferns and creepers hang down from the sides of the peaks and trees crown their summits. Man and nature are blended together; although the actual expression of the faces is not visible, mood and intention are clearly expressed by vivid gestures and movements of the legs and by bodily attitudes. We saw the same vivid sense of intention in the Sui plates in the last chapter. The fort in the middle right of the picture may be of Tibetan construction, for the pavilions over the watch-towers are different from those on the buildings to the left (cf. p. 161 above) and even those in the plate on p. 157 which are Chinese in style. *Cf. p. 66*

CAVE 217

CAVE 217

The plate on p. 157 likewise originates from Cave 217, and is evidently by the same artist as the plate on p. 155. This was thought to be the Fight for the Relics of the Buddha outside the town of Kuśinagara in India, where he died. However, Arthur Waley thinks it portrays the Buddha as Prince Siddhārtha (before he attained Buddhahood) watching the martial exercises of his clan.
The rows of soldiers contrast with the lines of princely figures on horseback at right angles to them. The solid walls of the town are counterposed to the trees rising vertically, treated with delicacy. The undulating landscape surrounding the scene completes the picture and make this one of the most brilliant landscape paintings in the world.

The lower plate on p. 161 forms a companion-piece to the plate on p. 157. It appears to depict a monastery with figures of monks by the door. Trees rise out of the inner courtyard where two central figures, possibly statues, are framed by decorated lintels. A willow-tree on the left outside the rear wall accentuates depth. This is the same technical device as was used in the Han relief in Fig. 33 (*Cf. p. 160*).

CAVE 45. Detail of the plate on p. 163

158

CAVE 45 (A.D. 713–762). Pages 158, 162–4

In these plates we see a wide stretch of countryside with a number of incidents taking place simultaneously which might depict the *Fa-hua Sūtra*. The composition appears to consist of successive zones produced by mountain ridges and hilly slopes; they are reminiscent of the earlier 'space cells' discussed above but are now wider and less rigid, leaving us with a sense of open space.

The unity of the whole is obtained by sloping diagonal lines and by the strong emphasis created by the dark rectangular tablets bearing inscriptions. This unity is reinforced by the intensive light which permeates the scene and gives a sense of depth.

The large plate on pp. 162–3 shows various episodes on land and at sea. The uppermost horizontal zone shows figures kneeling before Buddhas or Bodhisattvas; at the extreme right a man in white is placing a large tray of offerings before a Bodhisattva. These persons are evidently putting themselves under the protection of Kuan-yin. The seascape features a large boat with a black and white sail, bearing several people. (Cf. p. 158.) Lotus flowers float on the water while fish swim around the boat. Spirit figures are seen wrestling on the shore to the right; on the left shore is a tall tree with a man standing before it.

The plate on p. 164 is likewise a detail of the scene in the middle on the right; travellers emerging from a mountain pass meet others with pack-horses going towards it. Low shrubs (perhaps the dwarf oaks and pines common in mountainous regions) grow along the slopes.

The kneeling figures taking refuge with Kuan-yin surely also depict the *Fa-hua Sūtra*. Here we see clearly the new type of T'ang beauty inspired by the tragic Yang Kuei-fei; the women here are quite different from the tall slender figures in the Sui paintings. The landscape is a desert region with amber shading outlining the hills and banks. A delicate green, which is seen frequently towards the end of the T'ang period, becomes so characteristic of the Sung era at Tun-huang that we may almost call it a Sung green; brown, red and white are used for the robes of the figures. Fine lines and white are employed to high-light the folds of the robes. The rest is done in the shaded wash technique known as *mo-ku* or 'boneless painting'.

FIG. 33 – *Rubbing from a Han relief. The willow-tree on the right accentuates the depth. The same technique is also seen in the lower plate on p. 161*

Page 161 above (CAVE 217): detail of the plate on p. 155
Caption on p. 154

Page 161 below (CAVE 217): companion piece to the plate on p. 157
Caption on p. 156

Pages 162–3 (CAVE 45):
caption on p. 159

Page 164 (CAVE 45): detail of the plate on pp. 162–3.
Caption on p. 159

CAVE 205 (A.D. 713–762 and 763–820). Page 166

Two men are seen in animated conversation beside a mountain stream in spring. The brush-strokes are broad but have a soft and fluid quality. The figures are almost in silhouettes, reminiscent of those in Cave 323 (pp. 144f.); their gestures are intensely expressive. The composition follows a diagonal line from the middle background, sweeping down to the left and back across the picture to the extreme right of the foreground. Ferns grow by the banks of the stream and on the right a young tree gives a soft vertical line. In the background on the extreme left distant mountains and dark horizontal lines of clouds emphasize the sense of distance and space. The whole has an enchanting freshness.

The plate on p. 169 is a detail from the same cave (Cave 205), showing 'Meditation by the Setting Sun'. Here the technique of the boneless *(mo-ku)* method is applied in an accomplished manner. The entire composition is steeped in *p'iao-maio*, the floating or drifting light of a boundless desert plain. The colours are amber shades with black and soft green, giving an effect that is almost monochrome.

CAVE 320 (8th century). Page 167

The panel shown in the plate on p. 167 comes from the side of a paradise scene. It is a theme familiar in Sung poetry and in Ch'an (Zen) Buddhism: 'Meditation before the Setting Sun' (cf. p. 192). The colouring is mainly the delicate green already mentioned, while the countryside itself is executed entirely in the *mo-ku* or 'boneless painting' method. The perspective is such that the eye is taken to the distant horizon where the sun is setting.

conscious of the immensity of space, himself but a small unit within the whole. We also participate, identifying ourselves with him, moving as he moves, anxious about his reception in a strange city, thankful when he comes through a perilous mountain pass, silent and filled with wonder at a sunset.

The new vision of mountains that filled the paintings of the T'ang period started tentatively in the Late Sui. What the reason for this transformation was it is difficult to say. Perhaps there were several reasons: the development of Ch'an Buddhism; intensification of the cult of the Great Mountains, of Wu-t'ai Shan and others; the development and mastery of the sense of space displayed by artists like Wu Tao-tzŭ.

There were four steps to the painting of mountains: *kou* was the outline generally used for landscapes or mountains; *ts'un* was used to shade or model the contour lines (more about *ts'un* later); *jan* was to dye; *ts'a jan*, to apply a wash or tint of ink or colour in painting mountains, where the brush-strokes were not intended to appear; *hsi ian* was a wash shading from light to dark or one colour to another; *miao* was the outline of refined strokes to draw men and objects. The outline of peaks in a mountain range was *lun k'us (k'o)*, while rounded peaks piled up was *luan*. *Mo le* was the first outline of a peak which resembled blood veins, each one springing from the one before it, the nearest and lowest drawn first. *Chang kai* was the stroke that enveloped all the others and was the last outline of the complete peak.

We shall deal with *ts'un*, shading with brush-strokes, in the next chapter, as it occurs then. This is not to be confused with *mei ku*, graded colour washes, or other shading by colour wash. *Tien* (dots) were used for emphasis and clearer definition, and to indicate moss or grass on mountains and rocks; hence *tien t'ai*, the process of dotting rocks with moss.

Also important were the conception of a simultaneous vision; a wide stretch of countryside where various incidents take place at the same time, as indeed they do in life. This simultaneous vision is particularly associated with Oriental thought, where the emphasis is on the whole picture – on what we know to be there, not only

CAVE 205. *Cf. p. 165*

on what we see with our eyes, for 'the eyes can only see the limits, but not the whole thing.' Everything 'moves as time moves, but caught and captured as it moves through space, like a symphony: the mind plays an essential part, it is stirred with indefinable longing' (Waley).

CAVE 172 (8th century)

A favourite subject of painters at Tun-huang was Queen Vaidehī, who was imprisoned by her son. Amitābha Buddha appeared to her in prison and recommended sixteen subjects for meditation. Here we see her in 'Meditation before the Rising Sun'.

This landscape is perhaps one of the most coherent and the most developed in technique and execution. In the foreground the figure of the queen, holding an incense burner, is treated in the *p'ing-yüan* or level distance perspective (p. 103); thence one's eye is taken to the distant orb of the sun at the top left of the composition; the stream flows down the picture from the top right to the middle left and down diagonally to the lower right, opening out to the figure of the queen. The movement of the stream is emphasized and intensified by dark shading, first on the left bank and then lower down on the right bank. The water is shown flowing swiftly through a valley and pouring over boulders, giving the appearance of rapids, in almost the same manner as the water in our bronze basin (Fig. 13). The '*han-lin*', or leafless cold forest trees, provide an undulating movement across the picture from the left towards the middle. It is sunrise in early spring and this painting has all the charm that such a scene should convey. *Cf. p. 50*

CAVE 369 (*c.* A.D. 900). Page 173

These two landscapes are painted above the central paradise scene. The figures of the paradise scenes look grotesque due to oxidization of the blue and white colour used as a slip, which discoloured the original pink shading of the faces and distorted lines.

However, we are mainly concerned with the landscape. The immensity of the mountain ranges certainly seems to have been inspired by the mountains and plateaux of Kansu, stretching as far as the eye can see. The representation is akin to an aerial view. In this picture the *mo-ku* technique is used, with the trees indicated in the same manner as in the plate on p. 175. Dark washes of colour are employed for the series of plateaux, a typical feature of the Kansu landscape. Dramatic feeling is evident in the precipitous mountain walls and arid peaks; the light and dark washes of colour serve to bring this out extremely well. The whole effect of space is evoked cleverly and really conveys the atmosphere of a Himalayan mountain range.

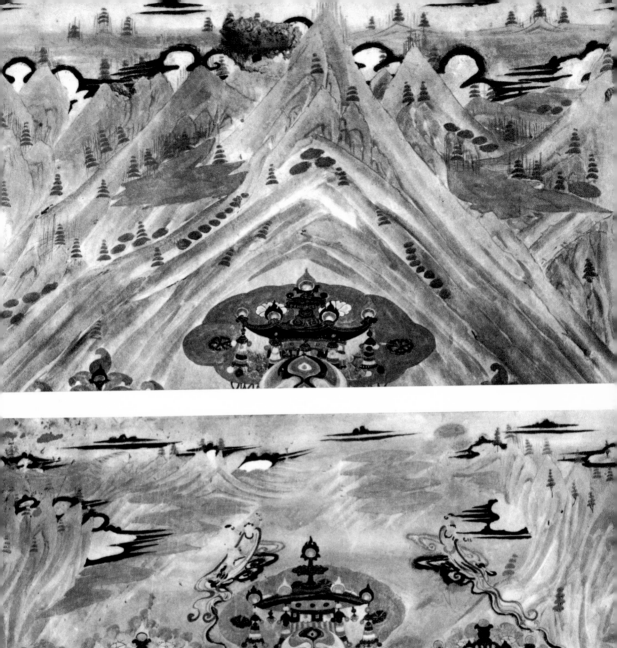

CAVE 198 (A.D. 581–617 and 960–1278)

In the right foreground before a bee-hive hut two men are holding by the arms a man clad solely in a loin-cloth; a horseman on a white mount and two other men kneeling beside him complete the group, set in a wide horizontal mountainous composition. Here the wash technique is used for the lower contours but the peaks themselves are outlined by a dark brush-line; the black clouds serve merely to give the effect of space, while the ground texture is produced by very fine *tien* distributed all over the picture surface, used in conjunction with patches of shading.

Page 174: detail of the plate on p. 176 (CAVE 112)

This cave belongs to the Late T'ang period; the painting, although representing a religious scene, is actually
a typical *fêng su jên* genre painting (one depicting
local customs, festivals etc.), and is a detail of a very
elaborate Paradise of the Bodhisattva Maitreya. It is
evidently a great occasion in the open air with noble
families attending. Arthur Waley says that the tower-
like structure on wheels, on the left, depicts the jewelled
throne given by King Śankha to Maitreya and by the
latter to the Brahmins who are here seen demolishing
it. Langdon Warner calls it a 'small temple on wheels',
while Joseph Needham points out that it resembles a
victory tower. Be that as it may, this pagoda, elab-
orately decorated with bells, tassels and flounces of
silk above the wheels (just visible below the flounce
along the base) is similar to the decorative architectural elements still found in many parts of the East.
They are usually taken on floats through the town
with dancers, singers and acrobats accompanying
them. There is a similar float on a Han tomb relief
at I-nan dated 193 B.C.; drawn by dragons (as
is quite appropriate for Han times), and with an
acrobat on its summit, it is preceded by knife-throwers,
flying carpets, jugglers etc.

In our plate on p. 179 we see two figures, possibly
Brahmins, on top of the pagoda, and similar figures
in front of it. A screened-off area (top left) contains
a long table with offerings of cloth and other objects
lying on it. In the screened-off area in the middle of
the foreground a tonsure ceremony is being performed,
while two horses – one white and the other a dark
bay – stand with a groom just behind. In a smaller
partially screened-off area three figures face a striped
tent, similar to those used for marriage feasts and the
like all over the East. Here a table is laid and guests
are shown sitting down to a banquet; other groups
of persons are kneeling or sitting on carpets spread
out on the ground.

The composition has been adapted to the unusual shape

of the space left by the paradise scene above. The ground is suggested by broad horizontal brush-strokes which contrast with the vertical lines of the stripes on the tent, the tablets and the tower; the carpet, tables and screens form oblique lines. The mixture of detail and simpiification which is a feature of most Tun-huang frescoes is seen here as well. The trees are rather curiously rendered: those in the background have a soft wash shading with *tien* indicating flowers; the carpets, the designs of the screens and the acrobats' clothing as well as other details are all carefully observed.

VI. THE SUNG DYNASTY (A.D. 960–1279)

> The breeze was almost imperceptible, the surface of
> the water calm . . . the moon rose over the eastern hills
> and began her lingering journey among the constel-
> lations. Her light fell like dew upon the sparkling
> river, which seemed to become one with the sky. We
> let our boat drift as it would, sailing over the vast
> expanse, and felt that we were sailing in empty space
> and riding on the wind . . . We were light as if we
> had forsaken the world, and free of all support like
> one who has become immortal and soars through
> space . . .[1]
>
> *Su Tung-p'o*
> (A.D. 1036–1101)

After the rebellion against the T'ang emperor Hsüan-tsung China
never completely recovered. Eight years of civil war depleted the
population. 'The sovereign already possesses a vast empire, why
should he wish to extend it still further?', sang Tu Fu, who expressed
the war-weariness of a whole population.

Perhaps this is the reason why the Sung dynasty is recalled with
such affection by the Chinese people, for they did not attempt to
conquer Central Asia. Innumerable operas, plays and epic poems
have been written about heroic episodes concerning members of
this family, for their military achievements were mainly confined
to defending their homeland from invaders.

After A.D. 960 the Sung rulers gradually united the country and
gave China stability for a hundred years, until Emperor Hui-tsung
tried to recapture a part of the country from the Liao people, who
had occupied it for a century and were in fact peaceful neighbours.
To do this he foolishly made an alliance with the rather savage
tribe Jurchen (Chin) of Manchuria. After the Chin had annihilated

---

[1] R. Grousset, op. cit., p. 198.

CAVE 321 (618–712, some parts repainted in A.D. 909–959). Page 183

This scene is practically painted in monochrome. A wide desert plain with sandhills takes up the whole width of this horizontal composition; in the foreground between the sloping hills, awaiting the order to ride forward, is a company of cavalry, their standards waving in the wind. The entire composition is in shades of amber for the desert terrain, and black and white for the figures and horses. Strong dark vertical lines are produced by the tablets, whose position bears an important relationship to the composition as a whole. This is a long way from the stylized Han mountain range in the plate on p. 37, but the basic idea of figures weaving in and out of the range of horizontally placed mountains is exactly the same as that common in Han times, such as we find in the masterpiece in the Boston Museum, 'The Entry of the First Han Emperor into the Capital of Ch'ang-an' (cf. p. 184). Even the standards on the left fluttering just above the tops of the hills are in the same technique as those in the Boston scroll. This is in fact nothing other than the old device in pre-Han and Han art whereby animals and figures were depicted in the act of emerging out of a mountain, thus producing the illusion of space and depth. The whole painting is executed in the *mo-ku* technique with some additional dark brush-strokes suggesting the textual surface of the mountains. It is a masterly work by a very great artist.

the Liao they advanced along the Yellow River, eventually driving the Sung to the south, where they established their capital in Hang-chow, while the Chin entrenched themselves as far as the Huai River. But a new menace came from the armies of the Great Mongol, Jenghis Khan. They began their assault in 1209. 'The sky was dark and filled with mournful sound' as they captured Peking in A.D. 1215.

The thirteenth century was one of great misery for China and the peasant population was reduced from a hundred million in 1125 to forty-five million in 1229. Later, in 1368, China was once again united under the house of Ming.

The Sung reign inaugurated great reforms under the brilliant leadership of Wang An-shih, who has been called a forerunner of modern democracy. Although the land remained in the hands of great landowners, he brought about much-needed fiscal reforms and abolished forced labour. Commerce was regulated by fixed prices; the state bought products and redistributed them in times of scarcity, keeping prices at a reasonable level. Wang An-shih said, as long as his reforms remained in force, 'rice became as cheap as water.' However, like everything else, laws need to be carried out by incorruptible men, and these reforms did not always produce the ends for which they had been inaugurated.

Public schools were established in every prefecture and sub-prefecture, and private academies developed where brilliant students were admitted even when they were too poor to pay the fees.

Books on philosophy, poetry, essays, history (the history of China from 403 B.C. to A.D. 959, the *Tzŭ-chih t'ung-chien*, was produced in 354 chapters) were produced in abundance; for block-printing, and printing by means of moveable type, increased the publication of books. A group of encyclopedists brought out volumes on geography, fiction and general knowledge. Treatises on ancient bronzes,

Page 184: detail of horizontal scroll showing entry of the first Han emperor into his capital Ch'ang-an. Compare this with the fresco on p. 183. *Museum of Fine Arts, Boston. Cf. p. 44*

CAVE 186 (A.D. 960–1278)

This is another of those details such as we have already seen in the plate on p. 169. On the left-hand side of the picture next to the halo of a Dhyāni Buddha, in which small Buddhas are painted, is a vast panorama of mountains and clouds steeped in *p'iao-maio* or floating light, with horizontal dark

stone tablets, foreign travel and commerce were beautifully illustrated. It seemed as if the three hundred years of the T'ang brought to fruition an extraordinary flowering of culture that has perhaps seldom been equalled.

During the Late T'ang and Sung periods the gradual unification of painting with poetry was completed: 'poetry is form and form is poetry.' A great deal has been written about Sung poetry and landscape painting; it is not intended here to go into detail. Nor is it the purpose to enter into a discussion already well advanced by others on the similarities between the French Impressionists and the Sung landscapists. It is said that Sung painting is 'sweet', that it cannot appeal to our present sensibilities, for, as Malraux says, it 'responds to nothing that torments us.' Perhaps one may disagree and think that precisely it does respond to that which torments us, only we may not be aware of it. It is true of course that we are inclined to like certain periods of art according to our own needs. But so few are aware of their own needs – whether 'conventional' needs or 'unconventional' ones, in the sense of material and spiritual needs (Watts). Are we not tormented precisely because we are mainly aware of the 'conventional' and shy away from the other, limiting our vision to 'that which the eye can see', not realizing that the eye cannot see the whole for its vision is limited?

Perhaps it would be useful to understand the difference between the attitude of the Sung painters and that of the French Impressionists. This is important because it involves the entire and profound difference between Asian art and European art since the Renaissance, and such an attitude permeates the whole history of Chinese art and landscape painting in particular.

The French Impressionists concerned themselves with imprisoning upon canvas the passing moment, the effect of light upon colour; bringing a sense of physical joy and well-being; seeking the tran-

clouds drifting across the sky, behind the range of mountains in the middle distance. The black shading used behind the mountains is new. As in the case of the plate on p. 169 not a single line is used in this painting, and the only colours employed are various shades of amber, black and white.

sitory nature of truth at that specific moment; lying in the sun on a summer day in a field full of poppies; eating wonderful French food; drinking sun-warmed wine; sailing down the Seine in a boat. The Sung artist was not in the least concerned to bring us this sort of passing moment. Using somewhat similar techniques and favouring certain abstract forms, he sought 'by the subtle choice of the fleeting moment to suggest eternity, while the mist into which he gazes swallows man up' (Malraux). For what he says in all his landscapes is, 'We are passengers of a day between earth and sky. Oh, to be the Long River that flows on for ever! To join with an immortal and fly away with him, to grasp the bright moon and live for ever! . . . But do you understand the water and the moon? This water that runs away is never gone, and the moon, though it waxes and wanes is never augmented or diminished. For if we consider things from the point of view of that which changes, then earth and sky pass away in an instant, but if we consider them from the point of view of that which does not change, then all things, and we ourselves, are immortal . . .'[2]

In Oriental art generally the personal is avoided and symbols are always sought to represent the essence of spiritual experience. This can be better understood if we realize how the artist was to prepare himself for his painting. The Taoist Chuang-tzŭ (300 B.C.) indicates that a painter should 'take off his clothes and sit cross-legged' – that is, he should be in the proper mental condition, free from all disturbing elements, as if he were to begin contemplation, or concentration on a spiritual truth; for 'when the mind is in repose it becomes the mirror of the universe, the speculum of all creation.'[3] Kuo Hsi (1020–90), the landscapist, in his 'Great Message of the Forest and Streams' says that everything had its 'secret rules' – how much more so in the case of painting. But how can it be expressed? 'Whatever motif the painter represents, large or small, complicated or simple, he should do it by concentrating on its essential nature,

[2] Loc. cit.
[3] O. Sirén, *The Chinese on the Art of Painting*, Peking, 1936, p. 51.

or the soul is not manifest.'[4] And his son, describing how his father settled down to work, says:

'On the days when he was going to paint (he would place himself) at a bright window before a clean table and burn incense right and left. He took a fine brush and the most excellent ink, washed his hands and cleaned the ink-stone as if to receive some important guest. He let the thoughts settle in his soul and then he worked ... with great care as if guarding against an enemy.'[5]

One thousand four hundred years separated Kuo Hsi the artist and Chuang-tzǔ the philosopher, but time did not change the fundamental conception of the moral and spiritual significance of a painting and an artist's attitude to his work. Kuo Hsi insists on the tranquillity of mind necessary to produce a painting of real inner significance, for the elements of landscape expressing the 'great drama of nature' are only the individual parts symbolizing the whole universe.

Chuang-tzǔ also emphasized this calm tranquillity of spirit, and he continually uses the image of the mirror, *le miroir spirituel* (Demié-ville), which by its very calmness attracts men. 'It is not running water into which men look (to see their reflections) but the calm still waters; they alone are capable of holding all those who stop to look; to reflect virtue man's spiritual mirror must be bright.' This same image is expressed by a Christian, de Fénelon, in 1699: 'Water which is agitated is not clear nor can it reflect the image of objects near to it, but tranquil waters reflect without alteration all images and retain none.'

In India water has always been regarded as a symbol of the divine. It took the place of an image in worship of the deity. 'In the symbolism of the myths to dive into water means to delve into the mystery of Māyā, to quest after the ultimate secret of life ... Boundless and imperishable, the cosmic waters are at once the immaculate source of all things and the dreadful grave' (Needham).

[4] Ibid., p. 45.
[5] Ibid., p. 46.

CAVE 288

This cave belongs to the Sui period but this painting – on the exterior wall over the entrance – is very Late T'ang or probably Early Sung. It has endured the desert sun and icy winds from the Gobi for eleven hundred years, yet the colour is still fresh although it must have been brighter originally. It

Let us digress a moment to examine the image of the mirror, for it has profound significance and is used continually in both Taoism and Ch'an Buddhism. The mirror image has been employed in all cultures: Hindu, Greek, Chinese, Islamic and Christian (Demiéville). It was first used, as far as we know, in the Hindu text of the Upanishad (500 B.C.). The Ātman, the inner-self or the Buddha nature within each living being, is assimilated to the reflection in a mirror.

'Just as a mirror which is covered with dust lights up like fire when purified, so also one who acknowledges the essence of Ātman reaches the goal of deliverance from sorrow.' The ninth-century Vedantist Śankara, himself a pupil of a Buddhist master, explains that the inner spirit (the Ātman) cannot be altered or changed by any effort on our part. If it remains hidden by our own ignorance it is still there 'as the brightness inherent in a mirror can be made visible by cleaning the mirror'.

The following verse and the answer to it made by the Sixth Patriarch of Ch'an Buddhism when he was only the illiterate servant of the Fifth Patriarch (638–713) is so often quoted by artists and critics in China that it must be given here.

represents a scene from the *Fa-hua Sūtra*, the theme of which is the dangers of the sea. A boat full of pious pilgrims, their hands clasped in prayer to their protector Kuan-yin, sails safely through waters infested by monstrous fish and dragons; on the bank devils are held back from pursuing them. From the clouds Kuan-yin, seated on a lotus pedestal, assures their safety. On the left a figure in white with clasped hands stands in a halo of flames. The boat is a typical example of Chinese naval architecture in that it has a broad stern and a bow, a transverse bulkhead construction and no keel. In all these cases the sails are atypical, implying that the usual 'slat' sails had not yet become dominant. The grain of the wood is rendered by fine wavy fibre-like lines. The four oarsmen are convincingly shown in arrested movement. The technique of *mo-ku*, used in the shaded washes of the hills, is here modified to *hsüan-jan*, a method in which shading is obtained by almost stratified marked-off light and dark zones.

The body is an Awakening Tree (Bodhi).
The Spirit is like a bright mirror;
Rub it incessantly so that it remains
clear and without dust.
The awakening has no Tree
And the Bright (spiritual) Mirror has no handle.
The Buddha nature is eternally pure,
Where then is the dust?

When the mirror is clear there is naturally no dust, when there is dust the mirror is not clear. This idea of contemplation before a mirror or before still water, both reflecting all things perfectly, PLATE P. 167 constantly recurs in Buddhist painting. In our plate we see figures in 'Meditation before the Setting Sun' and others sitting in front of pools of water, which will also reflect the setting sun, as indeed it reflects all things. For 'the Mirror is full of objects but in reality it contains nothing and yet appears to hold everything.' Thus the spiritual mirror must be clear, free from all disturbances; only then is the artist capable of bringing out the inner significance of his subject.

Kuo Hsi's essay on landscape clearly indicates that landscape itself is a state of mind. 'Mountains in spring are veiled in fleecy clouds, and people are happy. Summer mountains have shady trees, and people are contented. Autumn mountains are clear and pure, with falling leaves, and people are quiet. Winter mountains are covered by dark clouds and swept by storms, and people are silent and lonely.'[6]

Every alteration of distance causes a difference; the shapes of mountains vary with every step. A single mountain may combine the shapes and aspects of several hundred mountains. The clouds and vapours of real landscapes are not the same at the four seasons. 'In spring they are light and diffused, in summer rich and dense, in autumn scattered and thin, in winter dark and solitary...'

The shapes too 'depend on sunlight and shadow. Mountains without mists and clouds are like a spring without flowers.'[7]

[6] R. Grousset, op. cit., p. 196.
[7] Loc. cit.

CAVE 332 (A.D. 618–712 and 907–1368)

A charge by cavalrymen bearing lances is here placed in a horizontal composition set among mountains and clouds. In the foreground are the softly undulating sandhills of the desert which contrast with the violent, strong, swift lines of galloping horses and the long straight lines of the lances. A further contrast is between the dark wavy horizontal clouds on the right and the vertical *fêng* type of mountain on the left, consisting of peaks one behind the other drawn with thick brush outlines. The background has long horizontal brush-lines which emphasize space and the texture of the ground at the same time. This painting has all the powerful dramatic tension that characterized this type of battle scene from the Han reliefs onwards. *Cf. p. 65, Fig. 17*

This cave, which is one of the largest chapels at Tun-huang, was built, as an inscription tells us, in A.D. 960 by the 'third daughter of King Liu-tsê of the country of Sui-chien (Sinkiang). Li Hsin-tien has donated this cave in memory of her father. . .' The whole of the upper part of the rear wall is one panoramic scene of the sacred mountain Wu-t'ai Shan. It has been done in the form of a pictorial map, and gives a complete fresco of life in feudal China. The plate on p. 195, which is from the left end of the composition, is a view of the mountain peak itself, while the rest of the wall appears to be a detailed picture of the ascent up the mountain showing the various smaller peaks, passes, monasteries, pagodas, villages and roads found on the way. The lower part of the fresco seen in the plate on page 205 is taken up with terraced fields on the slopes of a hill being ploughed and sown; above it to the left is the mountain road coming out of a high-towered gateway; the inscription on the tablet near the gate says that it is 'the south-eastern road through the mountain gateway to the (province of) Hopei.' To the extreme right is a walled temple and above it a pagoda with a square base. The main storey has a rounded opening and an ornamental lintel above the entrance; three decorated corbelled roofs are surmounted by the traditional parasol of a Buddhist *stūpa;* bells hang from the roof ends with a rope for pealing them. Further up the mountain is a monastery, a timber-framed construction on a brick base with a tiled roof. In the walled courtyard a monk sits, probably chanting, while to the left of him a man is beating a gong and to the right two others stand in an act of devotion. The meandering zigzag road across the entire picture surface cleverly unites the various parts of the composition. The technique used is of the *mo-ku* type; the broad short horizontal brush-strokes indicate foliage on the trees; dark *tien* to the right of the fields are used to vary the surface and probably in this instance to denote low bushes; the mountains are contoured with broad brush-lines.

Wu-t'ai Shan is in the province of Shansi. As we have already mentioned (cf. p. 40), the cult of the sacred mountain grew in importance during this period. Wu-t'ai Shan was one of the most important of the five sacred mountains in China, and with T'ai Shan perhaps the largest. During the Chou period, *c.* 800 B.C., the mountain divinities were treated on the same footing as the highest officials of the court, the Three Dukes. In A.D. 725 the T'ang emperor Hsüan-tsung conferred the title of King of Heaven on the god of T'ai Shan, and in 1008 the Sung dynasty added to this title that of 'The good and saintly king equal to heaven'. It is with this growing cult in mind that we must look at the painting of Wu-t'ai Shan, 'The Five Terraces'. The cult of the Bodhisattva Mañjuśrī was started there by Emperor Hsiao Wên (A.D. 471–499). In the year 840 Ennin, the Japanese monk, visited its monasteries and saw a copy of the *Lotus Sūtra* in Sanskrit *(Saddharma Pundarīka Sūtra)*. He describes images of the Five Buddhas, each one between two Bodhisattvas, apparently in the style of Nālandā, the Buddhist university in Bengal, India. Pilgrims from all parts of the Buddhist world including India were then still making the journey to Wu-t'ai Shan. In fact a monk from the Tun-huang monastery made the pilgrimage about the same time as this mural was painted. If he brought back a map this would explain the map-like design in this fresco. *Cf. p. 40*

CAVE 61 (A.D. 980–995). Page 197

In some of the Late T'ang and Early Sung caves vertical panels are painted along the lower part of the walls in imitation of partitioning by screens. This vivid scene is painted in bright fresh colours, particularly green. Five boats with two-pronged broad bows and square sails are leaving harbour, with good spirits blessing their departure. The wind billows out the sails but the figures, their hands folded in prayer, are looking backwards. The shore is undulating and on an elevation is a statue (?) of a Buddha. He is shown with an elaborate nimbus and a halo decorated with a design of lotus petals, seated upon a large open lotus-blossom; figures are kneeling before an altar on which offerings are placed. Two Bodhisattvas with clasped hands sit on either side. Varying scenes follow in clearly defined spatial units formed by the hilly terrain and the triangular form of the shore. The inscriptions on the tablets cannot easily be deciphered. Once again this whole scene is executed in the *mo-ku* technique. The zigzag line of the shore runs vertically down while the black pointed two-pronged bows sharply accentuate the horizontal movement in contrast; a range of horizontal mountains at the back completes the composition.

CAVE 55 (A.D. 960–1278). Pages 198, 206, 207

Both the plate on p. 198 and the plate on p. 206 from Cave 55 depict a vertical panel from a series of imitation screen sections covering the lower wall surface. Three horsemen are riding out of a palace gate towards hilly terrain. The figure on the white horse is probably the Buddha as Prince Siddhārtha, portrayed as he rode out of his father's palace for the first time. The palace has been placed diagonally across the panel from left to right and the line of hills behind it runs from the right of the palace upwards and to the left, forming a triangle and thus breaking up the vertical panel obliquely; this effect is emphasized by the swift movement of the horses. The steeply-rising hills in the background accentuate the feeling of space created within this narrow format.

The plate on p. 207 from the same cave is a detail from another of these screen panels; it shows a very large boat which is again typical of Chinese naval architecture as regards the hull, but which has a 'bee-hive' hut built on the upper deck for shelter. The boat is leaving harbour; the piles of the jetty make a very interesting pattern in the composition which contrasts with the boat shown in movement. A Han stamped brick (Plate p. 208) representing a bridge uses the vertical lines of the piles in a similar manner; but in that case the contrast is with the swift movement of the horses on the bridge. Such a juxtaposition of heavy static elements and swift movement is frequently used in Chinese art. Our plate depicts the terrors of a sea voyage; in the sea monstrous fish are avidly awaiting the travellers and on the shore devils are delightedly dancing in expectation of disaster. The large number of people on board are piously praying, no doubt to their protector Kuan-yin.

At Tun-huang most of the later Sung caves repeat themselves in a rather compelling but monotonous rhythm of thousands of small painted Buddhas sitting in *dhyāni* or meditation. However, the earlier Sung caves of the tenth century show no signs of failing inspiration, and reflect all the main tendencies prevalent at the time.

Perhaps the three categories most popular at Tun-huang in the tenth century were *Tao-shih* (Taoist and Tao-shih Buddhist subjects), *Jên-wu* (human affairs) and *Shan-shui* (landscapes).

In the Jên-wu class the following groups are frequently seen:

Fêng-su jên-wu – genre painting, local customs, festivals etc.;

Shih-shih jên-wu – illustrations of authentic events or incidents;

Ku-shih jên-wu – illustrations of legendary incidents;

Shih-nü jên-wu – beautiful women.

We noticed that the two techniques, *kou-le* or contour line, and *mo-ku* or boneless painting were used in the plates of the T'ang period. *Ts'un* is to shade, *ts'un-fa* the general method of using *ts'un*. *Ts'un* as it developed became highly complicated, and has been translated as 'wrinkles', that is to say, it suggests the texture of stones, rocks, mountains, tree-trunks etc. However, we may describe it as *ts'un*, shading with brush-strokes and dots placed over one another giving the effect of texture. This is very different from *mo-ku*, with washes of colour alone. There are three main groups of *ts'un* containing twenty-five varieties of *ts'un*:

1. *p'i-ma ts'un:* brush-strokes like wavy fibres, giving the effect of eroded slopes and slight relief to the terrain.

2. *tou-pan ts'un:* short oval strokes of the brush said to resemble 'the halves of a split bean', applied vertically and done in pairs. They are usually used for the weathered slopes of mountains.

3. *hsiao-fu-p'i ts'un:* wide ragged strokes made by the brush being held sideways; they give the effect of greatly eroded rocks.

It was said that Li Ssǔ-hsün used the type known as *ma-ya ts'un*, resembling horses' teeth, applied with stiff hard strokes, which is a variety of this third group.

In our plates *ts'un* is generally used in a very early form. Apart from the different varieties of *ts'un* for effects of texture, *tien* (dots) were also used for this purpose. In Chapter IV we went into the details of *tien* used for trees and leaves. *Tien* were used on mountains and plains to emphasize contours and give the effect of distant trees, moss, ferns etc. There were also special forms of brush-strokes used to depict water. These varied according to whether they were to show springs, waterfalls, or long winding rivers through a landscape; there are strokes for rippling waves on shallow water, deep water with foam and spray; waterfalls suddenly changing course and flowing from a horizontal to a vertical plane; a stream flowing through a valley and pouring over boulders; a waterfall broken with clouds; a stream flowing on a level plane from one side to another; a stream disappearing behind a mountain or rocks and emerging further along, etc. Many of these methods can be seen in our plates, both in the Late T'ang and Early Sung periods.

The brush-strokes for cloud forms, thin light floating clouds, clouds used for breaking up mountains and so giving the appearance of depth and height, and other variations – all these are also part of the technique of painting landscapes. These techniques were developed and varied by different artists. The well-known landscapist Mi Fei, for example, used *ta-hun tien*, generally kept for painting broad leaves in full summer foliage, for his mountains as shading and this is therefore known after him as *Mi tien ts'un.*

CONCLUSION

It has often been asserted that the predominant influence at Tun-huang came from the West, from Central Asia and India. It is true that certain scenes were painted by foreign artists, and that specific decorative motifs may often show foreign influence, but in the main this influence is restricted to the iconography of the purely religious figures, such as the groups of the Buddha and attendants, bare-bodied, with the triple flexion movement of Indian art; the spirit of the paintings remains unmistakably Chinese. In the development of landscape external influence is negligible. A vivid elegant world of nature developed here quite indigenously; the characters move with a verve and ease that is peculiarly Chinese.

Continuous threads unite the Tun-huang frescoes with the fantasy and mythology of pre-Han and Han times. On these walls we see not only how Chinese art was used to depict the story of the Buddha, but also the development and perfection of Chinese landscape painting and the evolution of various techniques – composition, perspective and brushwork – sometimes down to the smallest detail. In fact, nothing less than the mainstream of Chinese painting can be studied at Tun-huang. The continuation into subsequent periods of certain elements of Late Chou and Han art, the mixture of fantasy and reality, the use of various forms of mountain and of trees and architecture, the development of vertical composition, and the actual technique of using the brush, particularly in the *mo-ku* or boneless painting which, if originally influenced by Indian technique, may well have developed here and spread to the rest of the country – all these make a knowledge of the art of Tun-huang an essential and vital factor in the understanding of Chinese painting. No one who has had the privilege of seeing the four hundred and sixty-nine caves can doubt that the prevailing character is native, whatever may have been borrowed from India and Central Asia.

For in Tun-huang we find 'the breath of the spirit that sings through the flaming rhythm of Han lacquers and Wei reliefs with a poignant immediacy'; this flaming rhythm belongs only to Chinese art.

While acknowledging the importance of subject-matter, iconography and other factors, it is only by studying the fundamental elements governing the development of an art that it can be truly understood. The indigenous forms of an art with strong traditions are born early; they are the very soul of the culture itself. Chinese culture and art are masculine and dominant in character, absorbing and transforming foreign ingredients into their own characteristic pattern. Such a culture chooses only those ideas of foreign origin which will thrive on its own soil, ideas to which it already has a predisposition. Let us try to exemplify this point by examining two early caves, 257 and 285. There is much controversy as to whether the artist of Cave 257 may have been a foreigner. However, there are innumerable elements linking the paintings with certain Han reliefs, and this idea cannot be accepted before further studies are undertaken. Again in Cave 285 part of the wall-paintings depict Indian Hindu divinities, and it is thought that the artist of these paintings may have been an Indian. However, no Indian artist in my experience painted Vishnu, Garuda and other figures in this manner. The whole feeling as well as the quality of the line are quite unlike those of Indian art, and in fact these figures blend so completely with the rest of the paintings in the cave, which are undoubtedly Chinese, that the suggestion is difficult to credit. Such theories remind one of the story of the Japanese artist Hasegawa, yelling in exasperation at the endless requests for explanation from his Western students, 'What's the matter with you? Can't you feel?'

Again it has been asserted that nearly all the art of Tun-huang, especially that of the earlier periods, was a provincial art. Study of the caves does not bear this out. Many caves may have been painted by local men who were not great artists, but this could be true anywhere, even in the capital. If the art of Tun-huang is to be dismissed simply as provincial art, without discrimination, then Chinese art in the capital must have reached a level never attained elsewhere in the world. The truth is that the importance of Tun-

Page 205: detail of wall-painting from Cave 61. *Cf. p. 194*

CAVE 55 (A.D. 960–1278)

The plate on p. 206 represents a procession of carts with decorated canopies entering a village; the upper part of the wall is taken up by a paradise scene. The inscription on the left says: 'The Great Divine Being Kuei (?) showing his supreme power at Li village'. In the left of the foreground, horses are being tended in stables; the walled enclosure in which people are standing is the courtyard of the village temple; at the top on the left is an enclosure fenced with wood. Above the landscape is an elaborate paradise scene, a detail from a long panoramic fresco. The whole is executed in the *mo-ku* method. The other inscriptions on the tablets have not been deciphered.

Page 207: CAVE 55. The way in which the supports of the piers are represented calls to mind the similar piers of a bridge on a Han stamped brick (p. 208). *Cf. p. 199*

Page 208: Rubbing from a stamped brick. Han dynasty. *Cf. pp. 199, 207*

huang as a centre of religion and learning – one has only to think of the size of the walled-up library – makes it probable that in many aspects of painting and sculpture it was a centre which gave a lead to the rest of China. This is supported by the fact that one of the Wei emperors transported thousands of artisans from Tun-huang, undoubtedly to excavate and decorate the Yün-kang and Lung-mên caves. A wall-painting found in a temple on the Wu-t'ai Shan mountain, near the capital and a thousand miles away from Tun-huang, seems to be exactly like some of the T'ang murals at Tun-huang; certain frescoes in the Mai-chi Shan cave-temples, also in Kansu, but much nearer the capital, forty-five miles from T'ien-shui, are not in any way superior to the Tun-huang murals. In fact some late Sui murals in Mai-chi Shan and a certain cave at Tun-huang have a great deal in common.

There is a prevalent suggestion that the T'ang caves at Tun-huang reached a high level of excellence, but that those of the earlier periods were crudely composed and were executed by second-rate artists. It is true that some of the earlier caves are inferior, but this is also true of some of the T'ang caves.

Of the two early caves discussed above Cave 285, with its extraordinary elegance and ethereal quality, is perhaps one of the most beautiful examples of mural painting in the world, and Cave 257 has a rich textural quality and inner strength. In front of these paintings one experiences the same sense of wonder and humility as with the frescoes in Arezzo, Assisi or Siena. The emotional impact of the best caves, including some of the earlier ones, is equal to that of the very greatest art.

One of the errors made in writing about these frescoes is to compare them with paintings on silk. Can one expect the brush-strokes on a plastered wall to be the same as those on silk? Yet they have been compared, without recognition that the essential quality of a mural is bold simplification. The problem confronting an artist when he faces a piece of silk, or a wall space, and often a whole cave, is entirely different, and the extraordinary sense of unity which some of the artists achieved when painting a whole chapel is of the highest artistic merit. Apart from the caves from which these landscapes have been taken, there are dozens of others where the constancy of the rhythm, often dynamic and inspired, and the balance of composition between the vertical and horizontal panels, and the globe-like appearance of the ceiling give them a brilliant homogeneity which could only be conceived by great artists.

Many scholars who write brilliantly on Chinese art forget that it does not represent a striving towards realism; when Professor Soper says that the dependence of the Chinese artists on the memory image 'retarded the progress of Chinese art towards realism' by 'the transformation of nature by the creative mind', by implication he imputes limitations of the same kind to all European pre-Renaissance art. Since it is precisely this 'transformation of nature by the creative mind' that has given us the greatest tradition of landscape painting in the world, it is permissible to ask whether the pursuit of realism has not been a limiting factor. The conquest of depth in painting, the achievement of three-dimensional effects from a static viewpoint, which occupied the talents of the Renaissance artists, has surely lost much of its charm for us because of its comparative immobility and rigidity. Today, 'in respect of art, we are the first to be heirs of all the earth.'

The essential form of this art, as of Gothic art in Europe, is that of juxtaposition without the limitations of linear perspective; the picture expands, revealing itself like a panorama. One of its essential qualities is that the beholder participates in the painting and identifies himself with what is represented. He must not remain detached for in doing so he would be able to grasp only part of the whole; he who sees 'only a single aspect of the Tao will not be able to comprehend its totality', and the meaning will escape him for it is uncontrolled, suggestive, mysterious, stimulating, and 'sharpens perception'.

This quality was mainly achieved through the treatment of space. In the 'hovering or dynamic view region' used by the Chinese artist, perspective corresponds to reality in the sense that parallel lines which in reality never meet, are not made to do so. The absence of geometrical perspective did not limit the Chinese landscapist in conveying what he wanted to express.

Analysis of the techniques used in Chinese landscape painting, though essential, will not give a complete understanding of the profound meaning it seeks to impart. The Chinese word *li* (principle) means the universal principle of order. It is seen in the formless, fluid, intricate patterns in jade and wood. In the universe there are *li* and *ch'i*. The *li* of the Tao pertains to 'what is above shapes' and is the source from which all things take shape. *Ch'i* is the material, the instrument. 'From *li* men and things received their natures; from *ch'i* their forms.'

'The Tao of Heaven operates mysteriously and secretly; it has no fixed shape; it follows no definite rules *(tsê)*; it is so great that you can never come to the end of it, it is so deep that you can never fathom it.'

The nature of Chinese landscape painting is precisely *li*; we must discover it, using not only the cold technique of logical analysis, but by *kuan*, or silent contemplation, for 'to a mind that is still the whole universe surrenders.'

APPENDIX

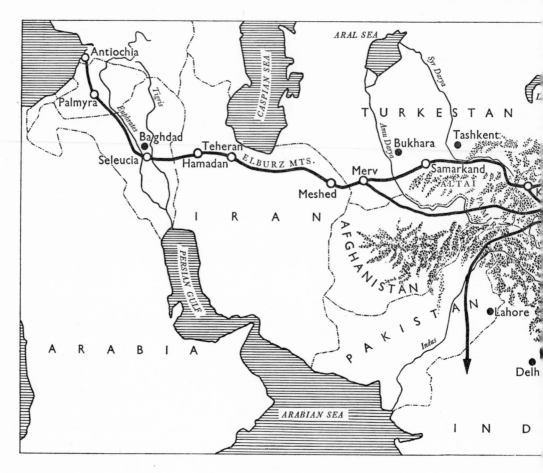

The Silk Road, the most important trade-route of the Orient, leads from China through Central Asia to Antioch on the Mediterranean; an offshoot follows the Indus to the plains of India. The chief articles obtained by the East from the trade along the Silk Road are glass, precious metals and cultivated plants (clover, peaches, almonds), while the West obtains silk and gold. The production of silk was very important already in pre-Han times, probably from the Shang period onwards. It was not only a desirable article of import for the West, but in China itself served as currency: taxes, for instance, were partly paid in the form of bales of silk. The quality of the fabrics was standardized, as were their breadth

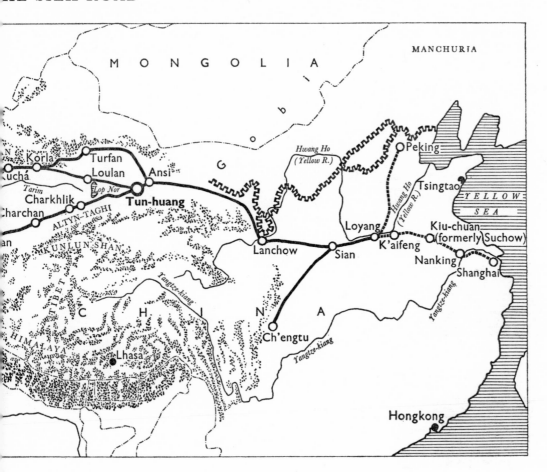

and length. The dissemination of Buddhist doctrine and culture also followed the trade-routes to a large extent. It was in the trading settlements that the first Buddhist communities in Central Asia appeared. Thus the oasis towns along the trade-route were not only centres for the distribution of goods but also the sites of Buddhist monasteries which transmitted to the peoples of Central Asia and the Far East the religious teaching and above all the wealth of artistic symbolism that had been developed in India. In these monasteries artists combined Buddhist concepts with Chinese art forms.

CHINA: HISTORY	CHINA: ART HISTORY	TUN-HUANG
B.C.		
200 HAN DYNASTY (206 B.C.–A.D. 220) Western Han (206 B.C.– A.D. 9) Edicts against literature rescinded (191 B.C.) Expedition of Chang Ch'ien to Central Asia (138–136 B.C.)	Chinese Middle Ages begin Buildings in wood and brick. Barrel-vaulting, cupolas and false cupolas, wall-painting Flourishing of silk industry; silk spreads to Korea, Japan and India	
100 Absolutist empire gradually gives way to theocratic cen- tralized state administered by a bureaucracy. Growth of the gentry Rebellion of Wang Mang	Clay funerary gifts preserved in huge quantities, also models featuring scenes of daily life Architectural models Bronze-casting Manufacture of paper from silk waste	Tun-huang founded on the Silk Road (105 B.C.) as a strategic base to protect the Great Wall
A.D. **0** Eastern Han (25 B.C.– A.D. 220). Capital: Lo-yang Economic and social reforms under Wang Mang (A.D. 9–23) Spread of Buddhism under Ming-ti (A.D. 58–75)	Development of ink drawings	Penetration of Buddhism Embassies from the West (A.D. 65)
100 Universities and provincial schools founded (A.D. 124) Rebellion of the 'Yellow Turbans' (168)	Decline of art and culture	
200 Disintegration of Han Empire Decline of traditional ways of life		

INDIA	KOREA - JAPAN	EUROPE	
			B.C.
Sunga dynasty in north India (185–72 B.C.)	Japan: Yayoi era begins (c. 200 B.C.)	Greece: Hellenism	200
Greek conquests in border area of north India		Rome: Republican period (510–31 B.C.)	
Sātavāhana dynasty in Deccan (c. 150 B.C.–A.D. 200)		Venus of Milo (c. 150 B.C.)	
Andhra art		Romans conquer Italy	
Saka on north-western border of India (from 130 B.C.)	Korea conquered by Chinese Han dynasty (108 B.C.). Kingdom of Lo-lang	Julius Caesar (100–44 B.C.)	100
Afghanistan: Gandhāra art under the Kushans (2nd cent. B.C.–5th cent. A.D.)	Korea: foundation of Silla (57), of Koguryo (37), of Paekche (18)		
		Roman Empire (75 B.C.– A.D. 480)	
Kalinga kingdom (Orissā), capital: Kalinganagāra (1st cent. B.C.–1st cent. A.D.)		Emperor Augustus (27 B.C.– A.D. 14)	A.D.
Kalinga art		Emperor Nero (54–68)	0
Mahayāna Buddhism			
Early Mathurā school			
Beginnings of Gandhāra sculpture		Emperor Trajan (98 –117)	100
Begram ivories			
Kushan and Mathurā art flourish			
Gandhāra stupas		Emperor Hadrian (117–138)	
Fire temple of Surkh-Kotal			
Roman factories in south India		Emperor Marcus Aurelius (161–180)	
Decline of Kushans		Soldier emperors (180–305)	
Late Mathurā style			
Pallavas invade south-east India (from c. A.D. 250)		Development of Germanic art and culture	200

	CHINA: HISTORY	CHINA: ART HISTORY	TUN-HUANG
200	THREE KINGDOMS PERIOD (220–265) SIX DYNASTIES PERIOD in the south (265–589) China partitioned Peasant revolts, civil wars, raids by Tibetans, Turkic Mongols, Huns and proto-Mongols Nanking becomes capital of the south Trade with Byzantium	Painters: Ts'ao Pu-hsing (c. 240), Chin Ming-ti (299–335)	
300	WESTERN CHIN DYNASTY (265–316) EASTERN CHIN DYNASTY (317–420) 16 illegitimate barbarian states in north (304–439)	Earliest Buddha figure in China (338) Painters: Wang Hsi-chih (321–379), Tai K'uei (to 395), Ku K'ai-chih (c. 344–406), Tsung Ping (375–443)	Tun-huang grows in importance as a centre of trade and Buddhist scholarship (from 350) Caves founded by monk Lo Tsun (366) Cave 257 (386–532)
400	China split between Northern and Eastern Wei empires (420–588) Embassy to Ceylon (428) Buddhists persecuted by the Wei (446–452) Wei expand to the west (447) Sassanian embassy in China (455) North China conquered by Turkic Mongols Lo-yang founded as capital of Northern Wei (494)	Yün-kang cave-temples founded Painters: Ku Chün-chi (c. 460) Lu T'an-wei (c. 440–500) Northern Wei promote art and temple-building	
500	Liang Wu-ti (502–550) Zen Buddhism founded SUI DYNASTY (589–618) China re-united again	Painters: Chang Sêng-yu (c. 500–550) Liang Yüan-ti (508–555) Promotion of art and literature	Cave 428 (520–530) Cave 285 (538–539) Cave 249 Cave 259 Cave 419 (589–618) Cave 423 (581–617) Cave 299 (end of 6th or early 7th cent.)

218

INDIA	KOREA - JAPAN	EUROPE	
Vakatakas in Deccan (c. 280–520) Guptas at Magadhā in north India (c. 280–530)	Japan: beginning of Tumulus period (c. A.D. 250)	Christianity: Catacomb Church	200
Gupta Empire (320–752) Early Gupta art (320–415) Chandragupta II (375–414)	Fall of Lo-lang kingdom Rule of Koguryo (313–668) Beginning of Buddhism (372)	Constantine the Great (324–337) Edict of Milan Acceptance of Christianity Christianity becomes state religion (381) Partition of Roman Empire (395)	300
Taruma kingdom in west Java (c. 400) High Gupta art under Kumāragupta II (415–455) Bagh: rock-cut monasteries Ajantā, Deccan: rock-cut monasteries 16–17		Great Migrations (375–568) Hun invasions (Attila) Battle of Catalaunian Plains (451) Frankish kingdom founded by Clovis (466–511) Theodoric the Great (471–526) Apogee of Gothic power	400
White Huns (Hephthalites) in north India (c. 500–530) Late Ajantā caves Early Chālukyas in Deccan (c. 550–757) Harshavardhāna (606–647)	Official introduction of Buddhism at Silla court in Korea (524) Beginning of Asuka period in Japan (552)	Rise of Carolingians Benedict of Nursia (529) Justinian I (527–565) Building of Hagia Sophia (532–537) Lombards in Italy (569) Pope Gregory the Great (590–604)	500

	CHINA: HISTORY	CHINA: ART HISTORY	TUN-HUANG
600	Hierarchy of officials		Cave 296 (*c.* 600) Cave 420 (*c.* 600) Cave 198 (581–617)
	T'ANG DYNASTY (618–906) Capital: Ch'ang-an (618) Agrarian reform (624) Wars against Turkic peoples. Conquest of Korea	Flourishing of art and literature. Classical Buddha statues: elegant movement in lieu of earlier stiffness. Secular art, with human beauty as leading motif	Cave 301 ⎫ Cave 302 ⎬ (early 7th cent.) Cave 303 ⎭ Cave 321 (618–712) Cave 323 (618–712) Cave 217 (late 7th cent.)
	Greatest expansion of power under Emperor T'ai-tsung (627–649)	Characteristic T'ang works: animal sculpture, esp. terracotta horses with legs turned inwards and polychrome glaze	Cave 103 (713–762) Cave 45 (713–762)
700	Chinese sovereignty over eastern Turkic tribes in Tarim basin Temporary rule of CHOU DYNASTY (690–705) in Lo- yang under Empress Wu Han-lin Academy founded (725–1911) Flourishing trade between Arabia and China	Architecture: pagoda occurs ever more frequently as a place of worship; usually poly- gonal ground-plan, brick or quarried stone, lavish plastic decoration, strong colours and curved roofs	Cave 205 (713–762 and 763–820) Cave 209 (763–820) Cave 172 ⎫ Cave 320 ⎬ (8th cent.) Tun-huang conquered by Tibetans (763)
800	Christianity penetrates into China Buddhists persecuted under Wu-tsung (844–845) Buddhist monks, scholars and patriarchs: Han Shan (577–654), Tao- hsüan (595–667), Hsüan-tsang (602–664), Hung-jên (601–674), Shan-tao (612–681), Hui-nêng (638–713), Hsüan-chüeh (665–713) Buddhist worthies: Shen-hsiu (668–760), I-hsing (683–727), Chien-chen (688– 763), (Kanshin)	Wang Wei (699–759), Ma-tsu (to 788), Hui-kuo (746–805)	Tun-huang reconquered by Chinese (848) Cave 196 (892–894)

INDIA	KOREA - JAPAN	EUROPE	
Eastern Chālukyas in Vengī (from 630)	Japan: beginning of early Nara or Hakuhō period (645)	Pippin I dies (640)	600
Late Gupta period (from 650–730)	Taika reform, Taika laws	Sutton Hoo burial (655)	
Rajput kingdoms in north India (from 650)	End of Japanese rule in Korea	Pippin II (680–714)	
	Korea: Silla destroys Paekche (663)	Irish high-crosses (from mid-7th cent.)	
Arabs conquer Sind (712)	Silla destroys Koguryo	and illuminated books (from approx. 680)	
	Beginning of Great Silla period		700
Yaśovarman of Kanauj (c. 730)	Korean art completely under Chinese influence	Charles Martel becomes mayor of the palace (714–741)	
Rāstrakūtas in Deccan (757–973)		Battle between Tours and Poitiers (732)	
Palace of Bengal (c. 765–1162)		King Pippin (751–768)	
Vatsaraja (775–800)		Charlemagne (768–814)	
Founder of Gurjara-Pratihara Empire		Carolingian Empire (from 800)	800
		Carolingian art	
Cholas in south India repeatedly raid Ceylon (9th–13th cents.)		Louis the Pious (814–840)	
		Treaty of Verdun: partition of the Empire	
Indochina: emergence of Khmer Empire, capital: Angkor		Louis the German (843–876)	
Upper Burma: Pagan Empire (from 850)	Japan: beginning of Late Heian or Fujiwara epoch (from 898)	Charles the Fat (876–887)	

CHINA: HISTORY	CHINA: ART HISTORY	TUN-HUANG
900		Cave 369 (*c.* 900) Cave 321 (907–959) Cave 332 (907–1368)
End of T'ang period (906), 8 years of civil war		
FIVE DYNASTIES PERIOD (906–970) in north China, TEN DYNASTIES in south	Painters of the Five Dynasties period; Pu-tai (to 916)	
		Cave 323 (960–1278) Cave 198 (960–1278)
Rule of SUNG DYNASTY in north China (960–1279). Empire re-united again. Civilian central administration, agrarian reforms	Flourishing of literature and art. Printing invented, academies founded, scholastic schools of philosophy (Neo-Confucianism)	Cave 186 (960–1278) Cave 61 (960–995) Cave 55 (960–1278)
1000	Sculpture: life-sized painted Lohan figures Painting: brush paintings, 'one-corner' pictures	
1100 Southern Sung Empire (1127–1279) Chin Empire (Jurchen) in north (1115–1237)		

INDIA	KOREA - JAPAN	EUROPE

900

Java independent (from 860)		Cluny founded (910)
Paramaras in Malwa		Saxon kings and emperors
(900–1300)		(Ottonians 919–1024)
Chaulukyas in Gujarat and	Korea: Wang-kon founds	
Kathiawar (950–1304)	Koryo (918)	Ottonian art
Chahumana in Rajputana	End of Great Silla period	
(10th–12th cents.)	(935)	Henry I (919–936)
Chandellas in central		Otto I (936–973)
India (10th–11th cents.)		Otto II (973–983)
Late Chalukyas in Deccan		Otto III (983–1002)
(973–1190)		Capetians in France (987–1328)

Chola art flourishes in south India		Henry II (1002–1024)
Indochina: Khmer art develops		Norman Conquest (1066)
on big scale, extension of		
Angkor Vat		
Bengal: Pāla renaissance		Gregory the Great (1073)
under Ramapāla		
Kashmir: last renaissance		
Mahmud of Ghazni conquers		St. Bernard of Clairvaux
the Punjab (1005)		(1091–1153)
Disintegration of Gurjara-	Japan: beginning of Early	
Pratihara Empire (from 10th	Kamakura period (1185)	
cent.)		

1000 (aligned with Henry II row)

1100

223

LIST OF CAVES

Cave No.	Date	Page No. of Reproduction
257	*c.* A.D. 500 and 386–532	77, 79, 81
285	538–539	*73, 94–95, 98, 99*
428	520–530	82, 85, *93 above, 96*
249	early 6th cent.	*87–88*
299	beginning of 6th cent.	*101*, 120–1
296	*c.* 600	108, 110, *111*
302	beginning of 7th cent.	*112*, 117, 118–9
301	early 7th cent.	*113*
299	end of 6th or beginning of 7th cent.	*101*, 120–1
420	*c.* 600	*114 above, 123 below*
419	589–618	*114 below, 123 above, 124*
303	early 7th cent.	126
423	581–617	128–9
103	713–762	137, *142*
321	618–712 and 907–959	139, *183*
323	618–712 and 960–1278	3, 144, 145, *151*
209	763–820	149, *152*
217	late 7th cent.	155, 157, *161*
45	713–762	158, *162–3*
320	8th cent.	167
205	713–762 and 763–820	166, 169
172	8th cent.	171
369	*c.* 900	*173*
198	581–617 and 960–1278	175
112	undated	*174*, 176–7
196	892–894	*178–9*
186	960–1278	186
288	Late T'ang or Early Sung	190
332	618–712 and 907–1368	193
61	980–995	195, 197, *205*
55	960–1278	198, *206, 207*

The page numbers in Roman type refer to the colour plates, those in italics to the monochrome reproductions

BIBLIOGRAPHY

CULTURE AND HISTORY

Chang Wu-hui: Zum Studium der chinesischen Geschichte empfohlene Werke. Hupei, 1956.

Chavannes, E.: Mission archéologique dans la Chine septentrionale. Paris, 1913.

Eichhorn, W.: Kulturgeschichte Chinas (with bibliography). Stuttgart, 1964.

Grousset, R.: The Rise and Splendour of the Chinese Empire, tr. A. Watson-Gandy and T. Gordon. London, 1952.

Hedin, S.: Die Seidenstrasse. Berlin, 1940.

Hermann, A.: Die alten Seidenstrassen zwischen China und Syrien. Berlin, 1910.

Hermann, A.: Die Seidenstrassen von China nach dem Römischen Reich, in: Mitteilungen der Geographischen Gesellschaft, 1915.

Herrmann, H., Lou-lan. 1931.

Hudson, G. F.: Europe and China. London, 1931.

Lü Ssu-mien: Geschichte der Sui-, T'ang- und Fünf-Dynastien Periode. Peking, 1959.

Maspero, H.: Mélanges posthumes sur les religions et l'histoire de la Chine. Vol. 3: Etudes historiques. Paris, 1950.

Needham, N. J. T. M.: Science and Civilization in China. Cambridge, 1954–.

Stange, H. O.: Geschichte Chinas von Urbeginn bis auf die Gegenwart, in: Geschichte Asiens, by E. Waldschmidt, L. Alsdorf, B. Spuler, H. O. Stange and O. Kressler. Munich, 1950.

T'ang Yung-t'ung: Geschichte der Buddhismus in der Han-, Wei-, Chin- und Nan-pei-Ch'ao-Periode. Shanghai, 1955.

Teng Chih-ch'eng: Die zweitausendjährige Geschichte Chinas. Peking, 1954.

Wilhelm, R.: Geschichte der chinesischen Kultur. Munich, 1928.

Yang Jung-kuo: Geistesgeschichte des alten China. Peking, 1955.

Yule, H.: Cathay and the Way Thither. 4 vols. London, 1913–1916.

BUDDHISM, RELIGION AND ART

Auboyer, J.: Composition and Perspective at Ajantā, in: Art and Letters, vol. XXII, 1948, pp. 20f.

Beckh, H.: Buddhismus. 2 vols. (Sammlung Göschen, Nos. 174, 770.) 2nd ed. Berlin-Leipzig, 1920, 1922. New ed. by Heimo Rau, Stuttgart, 1958.

Clark, Sir K.: Landscape into Art. London, 1949.

Cohn, W.: Buddha in der Kunst Ostasiens. Leipzig, 1925.

Conze, E.: Buddhism: its Essence and Development. Oxford, 1951.

Coomaraswamy, A. K.: Elements of Buddhist Iconography. Cambridge, Mass., 1935.

Coomaraswamy, A.: Transformation of Nature into Art. New York, 1934.

Cowell, E. B. (ed.): The Jātaka, or Stories of the Buddha's Former Births. 6 vols. Cambridge, 1895–1907, 1913.

Demiéville, P.: Le miroir spirituel. Paris.

Dutoit, J.: Jatakam: das Buch der Erzählungen aus früheren Existenzen Buddhas. 7 vols. Leipzig, 1908–1921.

Kirfel, W.: Symbolik des Buddhismus. Stuttgart, 1959.

Le Coq, A. von and Waldschmidt, E.: Die buddhistische Spätantike in Mittelasien. 7 vols. Berlin, 1922–1933.

Loran, E.: Cézanne's Composition: an Analysis of the Form with Diagrams and Photographs of his Motifs. Berkeley-Los Angeles, 1947.

Prip-Møller, J.: Chinese Buddhist Monasteries. Copenhagen-London, 1937.

Seckel, D.: Buddhistische Kunst Ostasiens. Stuttgart, 1957.

Seckel, D.: The Art of Buddhism. (ART OF THE WORLD Series.) Translated by Ann E. Keep. London, 1964.

Soper, A. C.: Literary Evidence for Early Buddhist Art in China, in: Artibus Asiae, Suppl. XIX, 1959.

T'ao Ch'ien: T'ao the Hermit. Sixty Poems by T'ao Ch'ien, 365–427. Translated, introduced and annotated by W. Acker. London-New York, 1952.

Waley, A.: Chinese Poems. London, 1946.

Waley, A.: The Poetry and Career of Li Po. London-New York, 1950.

Waley, A.: Zen Buddhism and its Relation to Art. London, 1922.

Ward, F.: The Lotus Symbol: its Meaning in Buddhist Art and Philosophy, in: Journal of Aesthetics and Art Criticism, vol. XI, no. 2, Dec. 1952.

Watts, A.: An Outline of Zen Buddhism. London, 1932.

Watts, A. The Spirit of Zen: a Way of Life, Work and Art in the Far East. London, 1936.

GENERAL HISTORY OF CHINESE ART

Ashton, L. and Gray, B.: Chinese Art. London, 1935.

Bachhofer, L.: A Short History of Chinese Art. New York, 1946.

Binyon, L.: The Flight of the Dragon: an Essay in the Theory and Practice of Art in China and Japan, based on Original Sources. London, 1911.

Binyon, L.: The Spirit of Man in Asian Art. Cambridge, Mass. - London, 1935.

Burling, J. and A. H.: Chinese Art. New York, 1953 - London, 1954.

Carter, D.: Four Thousand Years of Chinese Art. New York, 1948.

Chu Chieh-ch'in: Kunstgeschichte der Chin- und Han-Zeit. Shanghai, 1936.

Cohn, W.: Chinese Art. London, 1930.

Hambis, L.: Central Asia, in: Encyclopedia of World Art, vol. I, New York-Toronto-London, 1959.

Sickman, L. and Soper, A.: The Art and Architecture of China. (The Pelican History of Art.) London, 1956.

Sirén, O.: History of Early Chinese Art. 4 vols. London, 1929–1930.

Soper, A. C.: Life Motion and the Sense of Space in Early Chinese Representational Art, in: Art Bulletin, vol. XXX, 1948.

Speiser, W.: China. (ART OF THE WORLD Series.) Translated by George Lawrence. London, 1961.

Willetts, W.: Chinese Art. 2 vols. Harmondsworth, 1958.

CHINESE PAINTING

Acker, W. R. B.: Some T'ang and pre-T'ang Texts on Chinese Painting. Leyden, 1954.

Andrews, F. H.: Central Asian Wall-Paintings, in: Indian Art and Letters, vol. VIII, no. 1, 1934.

Andrews, F. H.: Wall Paintings from Ancient Shrines in Central Asia recovered by Sir Aurel Stein. London, 1948.

Auboyer, J.: L'influence chinoise sur le paysage dans la peinture de l'Orient et dans le sculpture de l'Insulinde, in: Revue des arts asiatiques, Paris, 1935, vol. 9, no. 4.

Binyon, L.: Painting in the Far East. 4th ed. London, 1934.

Bussagli, M.: Die Malerei in Zentralasien. Geneva, 1963.

Cahill, J. F.: Confucian Elements in the Theory of Painting, in: Arthur Wright (ed.): The

Confucian Persuasion. Stanford, Calif., 1960.

Cahill, J. F.: Chinese Paintings, 11th–14th Centuries. New York, 1960.

Cahill, J. F.: Chinese Painting. Geneva, 1960.

Cohn, W.: Chinese Painting. London, 1948.

Contag, V.: Die sechs berühmtesten Maler der Ch'ing-Dynastie. Leipzig, n.d. (1940).

Contag, V.: The Unique Characteristics of Chinese Landscape Pictures, in: Archives of the Chinese Art Society of America, vol. VI, 1952, pp. 45 ff.

Dubosc, J.-P.: A New Approach to Chinese Painting, in: Oriental Art, new series, vol. III, 1950, pp. 50 ff.

Dubosc, J.-P.: Great Chinese Painters of the Ming and Ch'ing Dynasties. Wildenstein Exhibition Catalogue. New York, 1949.

Fischer, O.: Chinesische Landschaftsmalerei. Munich, 1921.

Fischer, O.: Die chinesische Malerei der Han-Dynastie. Berlin, 1931.

Grünwedel, A.: Alt-Kutscha. Archäologische und religionsgeschichtliche Forschungen an Tempera-Gemälden aus buddhistischen Höhlen der ersten acht Jahrhunderte n. Chr. 2 vols. Berlin, 1920.

Hallade, M.: Sculptures et peintures de l'Asie Centrale: l'Art des monastères bouddhiques, in: Le Jardin des Arts. Paris, 1956.

Härtel, H.: Indische und zentralasiatische Wandmalerei. Berlin, 1959.

Kuo Hsi: An Essay on Landscape Painting. Translated by S. Sakanishi. London, 1935.

Lee, Sh. E.: Chinese Landscape Painting. Cleveland, 1954.

Mai-mai Sze: Echo of a Cry. (Autobiography.) London, 1947.

March, B.: Some Technical Terms of Chinese Painting. Washington, D.C., 1935.

March, B.: Linear Perspective in Chinese Painting, in: Eastern Art, vol. III, 1931.

Medley, M.: 'Certain Technical Aspects of Chinese Landscape Painting', in: Oriental Art, vol. 5, no. 1, London, 1959.

Munsterberg, H.: The Landscape Painting of China and Japan. Rutland, Vt. – Tokyo, 1955. Second printing 1956.

Priest, A.: Aspects of Chinese Painting. New York, 1954.

Rowland, B.: The Wall-Paintings of India, Central Asia and Ceylon. Boston, Mass., 1938.

Rowley, G.: Principles of Chinese Painting. Princeton, 1947.

Sakanishi, S. (tr.): The Spirit of the Brush, being the Outlook of Chinese Painters on Nature from the Eastern Chin to the Five Dynasties, A.D. 317–960. London, 1939.

Sirén, O.: Central Asian Influences in Chinese Painting of the T'ang Period, in: Arts asiatiques, vol. III, 1956, pp. 3 ff.

Sirén, O.: The Chinese on the Art of Painting. Peking, 1936.

Sirén, O.: A History of Early Chinese Painting. 2 vols. London, 1933.

Soper, A. C.: Early Chinese Landscape Painting, in: Art Bulletin, vol. XXIII, 1941.

Sullivan, M.: On the Origin of Landscape Representation in Chinese Art, in: Archives of the Chinese Art Society of America, vol. VII, New York, 1953.

Sullivan, M.: Pictorial Art and the Attitude toward Nature in Ancient China, in: Art Bulletin, vol. XXXVI, 1954.

Sullivan, M.: The Birth of Landscape Painting in China. London, 1962.

Swann, P. C.: Chinese Monumental Art. London, 1963.

Waley, A.: An Introduction to the Study of Chinese Painting. London, 1923.

White, W. C.: Chinese Temple Frescoes. Toronto, 1940.

Yü Chien-hua: Geschichte der chinesischen Malerei. Shanghai, 1959.

MONOGRAPHS ON TUN-HUANG

Fourcade, F.: La peinture murale de Touen-Houang. Paris, 1962.

Gray, B.: Buddhist Cave Paintings at Tun-huang. London, 1959.

Hsieh Chih-liu: Tun-huang yi-shu hsü-lu (Descriptive Catalogue of Tun-huang Art). Shanghai, 1955.

Matsumoto, E.: Tonko-ga no kenkyū (Studies on the Paintings of Tun-huang). Tokyo, 1937.

Mizuno, S. and Nagahiro, T.: Yün-kang: the Buddhist Cave-Temples of the Fifth Century A.D. in North China. 16 double vols. Kyoto, 1952–.

Pelliot, P.: Les grottes de Touen-Houang. 6 vols. Paris, 1914–1924.

Stein, Sir M. A.: Ruins of Desert Cathay: Personal Narrative of Explorations in Central Asia and Westernmost China. 2 vols. London, 1912.

Stein, Sir M. A.: The Thousand Buddhas: Ancient Buddhist Painting from the Cave-Temples of Tun-huang. London, 1921–1922.

Tun-huang Pi-hua-chi (Collection of Wall-Paintings from Tun-huang). Place and date of publication and editor not stated.

Waley, A.: Ballads and Stories from Tun-huang. London, 1960.

Waley, A.: A Catalogue of Paintings recovered from Tun-huang by Sir Aurel Stein. London, 1931.

Warner, L.: Buddhist Wall-Paintings: a Study of a Ninth-Century Grotto at Wan-fo-hsia near Tun-huang. Cambridge, Mass., 1938.

INDEX

The numerals in italics refer to the plates and figures.

abstract motifs 40, 46, 188
Academia Sinica 12
academies, private 185
acrobat 19, *178-9*
aesthetic theory 83
Ajantā 34, 143
Alexandria 16, 134
alfalfa 54
al fresco technique 25
aloe 134
altar *197*
amber 19
Amitābha Buddha *171*
animals: at court 107; motif 42, 45, 62, 64, 83f., *108*, 116, *183*; mythical 16, 46; cf. *under individual species*
Annam 105, 133
apsaras 46f., *51, 132*
arabesque *113*
Arabs 19, 133
arch *118-9*
archaeologists 23, 56, *118-9*
archaism 10, *96*
archer, archery 39, 46, *73*, 84, *120-1*
architectural elements *44-5, 48*, 65, *69*, 90, *101*, 106f., *114*, 140, 147, *155, 178-9*, 202; cf. arch, balustrade, bridge, gallery, house, hut, pagoda, pavilion, roof, shrine, temple, terrace, wall, window
Arezzo 210
arrow-heads 22
artisans 61, 78, 210
artists 133, 211
Asia, Central 15, 19, 26, 30f., 54, *96*, 133, *151*, 181, 202; South-east *96;* Asian approach to art 33, 35, 187
Assisi 210

Assurbanipal *38*
Assyria *38, 52*
astronomers *53*
Ātman 191
Auboyer, J. 34, 143
Avalokiteśvara *124*

Bactria 15
balustrade 106, *110, 118-9*
bamboo 54, *82, 83, 98, 101, 118-9, 124*, 127, *137*
banner 16
battle scene *65, 193*
bee-hive hut *175, 207*
bell *178-9, 205*
Benares 77
Bengal *195, 205*
Biographies of Eminent Women (Liu Hsiang) 22
birds 40, 42, *44-5*, 47, 62, 64, 67, *73*, 77, 80, 83, *114*, 116, *139;* cf. *under individual species*
boar 42, *93, 139*
boat 61f., *63*, 64, *118-9, 145*, 147, *151, 162-3, 178-9*, 181, 188, *190, 197, 207*
Bodhi 26, 192
Bodhidharma 78
Bodhisattvas 29, *117, 124, 162-3, 178-9, 195, 196, 205*
boneless painting: cf. *mo-ku*
Bonin 22
Boston Museum 44, 66, *183*
Bouchier, G. 19
box 22, 89, *101*
Brahmi language 26
Brahmin *96, 178-9*
Braisted, P. 13
brick, stamped *37*, 54, *55*, 56, 61, *62, 63*, 63ff., 66, *69, 208*

229

bridge   140, *208*

British Museum   84, *123*, 140, *141*

bronze: arrow-head 22; mirror 45, *48*, 67, *130;* object 42; trade in 15; tube *47;* vessel 47, *48*, 50, 63, 106, *130*, *171*

bronzes 30f., 33, 40, 42, 45, *102*, 185; cf. 'hunting bronzes'

Buddha 19, 29f., 47, 77, *81-2*, 84, *93*, *96*, *98*, *114*, *118-9*, *123-4*, 133, *149*, *151-2*, *162-3*, *186*, 191, *195*, *197-8*, 202, *205-6;* cf. Amitābha, Dhyāni

Buddhism, Buddhist 54, 80; art 78, *96*, *98;* iconography 10; missionaries 75, 78; sacred mountains 40; pantheon 65; painting 30, 83f., *192;* stūpa 143, *205;* teaching 19, 26; Buddhists 19, 36, 78, *96*, 133, 140, 191; cf. Ch'an

Buhot, J.   12, 107

burial-place   *18*

bush   *195*, *205*

Byzantium   19

calendar   22

calligraphy   22, 39f., 46, 50, 67

camel   *108*, *118-9*, 134

camphor   134

canal   105f., 134

canopy   *123*, *124*, *206*

Canterbury Psalter   89

Canton   75, 78, 133, *151*

caravan   15f., *108*, 134

carpet   *178-9*

cart   23, *118-9*, *206*

caves 78; dating of 10; featured in painting *152;* cf. India, Kinnarī, Lung-mên, Mai-chi Shan, Tun-huang, Yün-kang

Caves of a Thousand Buddhas   12, *18*, 23

cedar   127

Celestial Mountains: cf. T'ien Shan

ceremony   42, *42*, 65, *178-9*

Ceylon   133

Ch'an Buddhism   39, 78, 135, *167*, 168, 191

Ch'ang-an   84, 105, 107, 133f., *184*

Chang Ch'ien   54, *151*

chang-fa: cf. composition

Chang Hêng   56

chang kai   168

Chang Sêng-yu   31

Changsha   *87-8*, *106*

Chang Shu-hung   12

Chang Yen-yüan   83, 143

charcoal drawing   *152*

chariot 43, *46*, *68*, *123*, *126;* charioteer, charioteering 39, *46*, *126*

Chavannes, E.   *68*

Chêng Tê-k'un   12, *93*

ch'i   35, *212*

Ch'i, Northern, art   45

Chiao-chih   75

ch'iao-chih   *116*

Ch'ien-fo Tung: cf. Caves of a Thousand Buddhas

Chin dynasty *82;* cf. Jurchen

ch'in   105

China, north 78, 105; south 105, 133; approach to art 33, 56, 91, 187, 189; approach to nature 36, 39, 41, 61; archaeologists 56, *118-9;* folk-songs 19; history, historians 56, 75; influence on Central and southern Asia 31; language 26; literature 12, 22, 26, 36, 39f., 53, 56, 135, 181, 185; painting 33f., 35f., 39, 43f., 63, 67, 83, 211f.; travellers 19

Ch'ing dynasty   26

Ch'ing-lu shan-shui   140

Ch'ing-pi shan-shui   140

Ch'ing-ping Hsien   *93*

ch'in-shou   83

Chin-ts'un   *102*

Chiu-ch'üan   20, 23

ch'iu ho   89

Chou *195*, *205;* Late   *41*, 42, *43*, *46*, 47, 202

Christians   19, 189, 191

Ch'üan-chou   133

Chuang-tzǔ   67, 188f.

Chu-chüeh 22
Chun Tsung *151*
Ch'u Yüan 40
civil service 53
Clark, Sir K. 39, 89
clay *37, 49, 52, 64*
cloth *178-9*
clothing 16, 19, 40, *126, 132,* 134, *151, 164, 175, 178-9;* cf. *dhoti*
cloud motif 40, 42f., 46, 55, *66,* 70, 80, *86-8, 98, 101,* 140, *155, 166, 175, 186,* 192, *193,* 201; cloud-mountain motif 43, 45, 89, *113;* cloud-scroll 30, 42f., *44-5,* 61
comb 22, 83, 134
commerce 15f., 26, 54, 133f., 185, 187
compass 25
composition 89f., *98,* 140, 143, *149, 166, 176-7, 178-9, 183, 193,* 202
Confucianism 36, 39, 53, 80
Coomaraswamy, A. K. 35
coral 16
cotton 16
court, imperial 53, *73,* 84, 107, 140; officials at 41, *195, 205;* ceremonies at 65
creeper *137, 155*
crystal 19
Cubists 35
customs *178-9,* 200

dance, dancers 30, *178-9*
Darbois, D. 9, 12
deer 42f., 45, *93, 98, 120-1;* deer king 77
Degas, H. G. E. 93
deities 41, *68,* 189, 203; cf. T'ai Shan
Delhi 77
Demiéville, P. 189, 191
demons 56, *82, 113, 190*
desert *3,* 15f., 153, *164, 169, 176-7, 183, 190, 193*
dhoti 77, *101, 117, 139*
Dhyāni Buddha *186,* 200
dice 22

documents 22
dog 42, 56, *93*
donor 26, *126*
door 106, *110, 117*
dragon 16, 40, 42, 55, 83, *87-8, 90, 101, 102, 178-9, 190*
drawing 25, 47, 64f., *87-8, 93,* 107, 152; cf. *po-hua*
duck 62; duck-hunting 61, *62,* 64f.
dwarf oak *164*

eagle 89
earth 55, 62, *87-8,* 89, 188
Egypt 16, 65, 71, 134
elephant 16, *96, 137, 139,* 147
El Greco *98*
elm 26, 105
embroidery 40
encyclopedia 185
Englishmen 22
engraving *47,* 65, *109*
Ennin *195, 205*
'Entry of the . . . Emperor into . . . Ch'ang-an' 44, *183*
envoys *133, 151*
Erh Ya 40
essay 185, 192
Europe 15, 22, 35ff., *93, 98;* European approach to art 33; art 35, *98,* 103, 187f., 211; cf. Greece, Italy
explorers 22f.

Fa-hua Sūtra *124,* 147, *158, 162-4, 190*
falcon 134
fan-tsu 83
Fénelon, F. de 189
fêng *193*
fêng su jên *178-9*
fêng-su jên-wu 200
Ferghana 23, 134
ferns *137, 155, 166,* 201
festivals 106, *178-9,* 200; cf. ceremonies

filigree 83
fir-tree 127
fish 83, *162-3, 190, 208*
Five Classics 39
'Five Terraces' *195, 205*
flame motif *98, 114,* 116, *190*
flax 16
fleur-de-lys motif 19
flowers 80, 83, *98, 104,* 118-9, *178-9;* cf. poppy
'flying gallop' 42f., *93*
folklore 10
folk-songs 19
footwear 16, 22
foreshortening *151*
forest *40, 98,* 105, 116, 133; fear of 36f., 39
fortification 20, 22, 30, *155*
Fountain of Wine 20
Freer Gallery of Art 45
French 22, 187f.
frieze 66, *98, 120-1*
'Frozen Pearl' 140
fruit 54, 83
Fukien province 105
funerary slabs *77;* urn *41*
fur 15f.
fu-sang *131*
Fu Tu 134

gardens 16
galleries 140
Garuda 203
gazelle 23
Genoese 22
genre painting *178-9,* 200
glassware 16
Gobi 13, 23, *190*
gold inlay *43, 47;* golden statue *151;* goldsmith 19
gong *205*
goose *64*
gorge 30
Gothic art 211

grain 16
grapes 54
grass 168
'Great Message of Forest and Streams' 188
Great Wall 15, 19f., 23, 105
Greece 26, 71, 191

halo 25, *98, 186, 190, 197;* cf. nimbus
Han: architectural elements 140; art 44, 47, 53, 55, 65, 70, 80, *82, 87-8, 183,* 202; brick *37, 55, 62, 63, 69, 208;* dynasty 20, 33, 53-74, *184;* empire 19, 75; excavations 56; funerary slab *77;* garrison 22; hunting scene 44, *52;* lacquer *87-8,* 203; mythology 202; painting 39, 56, 63, 66f., 107, *183;* panel *68-9;* philosophy 55, *86-7;* poetry 54; reliefs *42-5,* 65, *77, 82, 87-8, 90, 93, 98, 101, 104, 108, 160-1, 178-9, 193,* 203; tile *49, 64;* tomb *41,* 42, 56; watch-tower 22; cf. Chang Ch'ien, Ho Ch'ü-ping, Wu Ti
Hang-chow 105f., 133, 185
han-lin 63, 116, *171*
hare *93*
Harsha of Kanauj *137*
harvest scene 61, *62*
Hasegawa 203
head-dress *149, 155*
heaven 62, *87-8,* 89, 188, 212
Hedin, S. 22
hemp 16
hills *3,* 61f., 64, 76, *82,* 106, *114,* 116, *118-9, 123, 128-9,* 133, *143, 151, 155, 158, 162-4,* 181, *183, 190, 198, 205, 206;* cf. mountains
Hindus 19, 191, 203
historians 56
historical scene 147
Ho Ch'ü-ping 20, 77
Hōkiji *3*
Honan province 22
Hopei province *58-9,* 66, 107, *205*
horn 83
horse 56, *64,* 70, *82, 93, 101,* 107, *108, 111,*

118-9, 134, *137*, *139*, 147, *151*, *174*, *176*, *178-9*, *183*, *193*, *198*, *206*, *208*

horseman 16, 30, 43, *82*, *118-9*, 177, *183*, *193*, *198*, *206*

Hōryūji	147
house	*117*
Hsia Nai	12
hsiao-fu-p'i ts'un	200
Hsiao Wên	*195, 205*
hsi (ch'i) chien hên i fa	47
Hsieh Ho	35, 83
hsien	34
Hsien-wên Ti	78f.
hsi ian	168
hsin	39
hsiu shih	89
Hsi Yü Chi	*96*
hsüan-jan	*190*
Hsüan Tsang	13, 16, *94-5*, *137*, *155*
Hsüan-tsung, Emperor	134, 181, *195, 205*
Hsü Tao-ning	*103*
hua	39f.
Huai River	185
hua-niao	*83*
Hui-tsung, Emperor	83, 181
Hung Jên	24
Huns	19, 75
'hunting bronzes'	50, *57*, *82;* cf. duck

hunting scene *38*, 44, 50, *52*, 65, *82*, *93*, 107, *120-1*

huo-yen chih	116
Impressionists	187f.
I-nan	*41, 42, 178-9*
incense 189; -burner	*171*
incrustation	*101*

India 13, 15f., 31, *137*, *157;* northern 77; Indians 19, 77;
— , Indian, *apsara 51;* art *96*, *118-9*, 143, 202; art theory 35; cave-temples 34; deities 203; influence on China 31, 46, 202; Jain MSS 31; king 137, *151;* literature 36; missionaries 75; monks 133; philosophy 39; symbolism 189; trade with 54, 134; university *195, 205*

Indonesia	31; cf. Java
ink	*49*, 53, 67, 83, 168, 189
inlay	42, *43*, 47, *102*

inscription 22, 29f., *151*, *158*, *162-4*, *195*, *197*, *205*, *206*

Introduction to Study of Chinese Painting (Waley) 107

Iran	31, 44, 54, 61, *98*, 133f.
Islam	133, 191
Italy	22, 24, *28*
ivory	16
jade	15f., 41, 54, 134, 212
Jade Gate	15, 22f.
Jain MSS	31
jan	168

Japan, Japanese *3*, 133, 135, 147, *195*, 203, *205*

Jātakas 84, 147; cf. Mahāsattva, Ruru, Suddhanta, Viśvantara

Java	31, *118-9*
Jenghis Khan	185
jên-wu	83, 200
Jerusalem	134
Jīva, Princess	19
jugglers	19, *178-9*
Jurchen	181, 185
K'ai-pao	29
K'ai-yun	29
Kansas City	116
Kansu	9, *98*, *173*, 210
kaolin	25
kao-yüan	*91*
Karakorum	15
Kashgar	15, *137*
Kashmir	133
Khotan	15f., 29, 54
Kiangsu	22
Kinnarī	*132*

knife-throwers 178-9
Korea 54, 133, 135
kou 168
kou-le 137, 153, 200
kou-le-t'ien-ts'ai 153
Kropotkin, P.A. 22
kuan 212
Kuang Ya 39f.
Kuan-yin 29, *124, 162-4, 190, 208*
Kuchā 15, 19, *132*
Kuei *206*
Ku K'ai-chih 31, *73, 74, 84,* 89
Kumārajīva 19
Kumtura *132*
kung-shih 83
K'un-lun 15
Kuo Hsi 33, 89, *103,* 188f., 192
ku-shih jên-wu 200
Kuśinagara *157*
Kyzyl 15, *132*

lacquer 15, 40, 42, 67, 70, *87-8, 96,* 106, *106, 130*
lake 61f., *63,* 90, 106, 134, *149*
lance *193*
leather 22
legends 41
lemons 54
Leonardo da Vinci *93*
leopard 42
Li *206*
Liang dynasty *151*
Liang Wu-ti 78
Liao 181, 185
Liao-yang 56
library 210
Li Chao-tao 135, 140
Li Hsin-tien *195, 205*
Li Kuang-li 23
ling-chih 45
lion *101, 139*
Li Po 19f., 105, 134f.

Li Ssŭ-hsün 135, 140, 200
literature: Chinese 12, 22, 26, 36, 39f., 53, 56, 135, 181, 185; European 36; Indian 36; cf. encyclopedia, essay, play, poetry
Liu Hsiang 22
Liu Pang 53
Liu-tsê, King *195, 205*
Lohans *151*
Lo-lang 47
Lo Tsun 24
lotus 61f., *63,* 70, *124,* 144, *162-3, 197;* -pond 30, *98, 114, 124;* throne *117, 123*
Lotus Sūtra 124; cf. *Saddharma Pundarīka Sūtra*
Lo-yang *49,* 78, 80, 84, *102,* 105f.
luan 168
Lu Chu Yung 15
Lung-hai 20
Lung-mên caves 78, 80, 210
lung-yu 83
lun k'us 168
Lust, J. 12f.
lute 71

Mahāsattva *82, 85, 96;* Jātaka *82, 93*
mahout *137*
Mai-chi Shan 9, 12, *98, 113,* 210
Maitreya *178-9*
Mallikā *96*
Malraux, A. 187f.
Manchuria 56, 181
Manicheans *133*
Mañjuśrī *114, 195, 205*
manuscripts 26, 31
mao-lin *63*
Māra *82*
Marco Polo 16
marriage feasts *178-9*
masks *139*
Maspero, H. 53
Māyā 189
ma-ya ts'un 200
medallion *143*

meditation *169, 171, 176-7,* 192
Medley, M. 61
mei ku 168
memoirs 13, 19
merchants 26, 30, 66, 133; cf. commerce
metal 55; box 89, *101;* objects 42; cf. bronze, gold, silver
miao 168
Middle East 15, 134; cf. Assyria, Iran, Syria
Mi Fei *3,* 201
Ming dynasty 185; Gate *17,* 24
Mirān 15
mirror 45, *48,* 67, *130,* 188f., 191
missionaries 75, 78
mi tien ts'un 201
Mo-ch'i 140
mo-chu 83
mo-ku 107, *118-9, 144, 145, 151,* 153, *164, 167, 169, 173, 183, 190, 195,* 200, 202, *205, 206*
mo le 168
monasteries 25f., *161, 195, 205;* Monastery of Eternal Peace 80
Mongols 19, 75
monks *18,* 24, 78, *81,* 84, *98, 124,* 133, *137, 151, 152, 161, 176-7, 195, 205*
monsters 40, 56
moon 89, 105, 181, 188; instrument for measuring 53
moss 168, 201
mountains *3,* 30f., 34, 36, 40ff., 47, *48,* 62, *69,* 70, 80, 83f., *87-8,* 89f., *98,* 107, *137, 139,* 140, 143, *145, 149, 152, 158, 162-4,* 168, *173, 175-7, 183, 186,* 192, *193, 197,* 200, 201f.; cult of 168, *195, 205;* cf. cloud-mountain, *hsien and under individual mountains*
'Mount Lu' 91
Mu-lan 80
music, musicians 39, 47; musical instruments 30; cf. gong, lute, opera
Mycenaean *93*
Myngoo Wong 12
mythology 65, *87-8, 96,* 202; cf. legends

Nālandā *195, 205*
Nanking *73,* 75, *84*
Nan Shan 23
Nara *3*
Needham, J. 12, 19, 53, *178-9,* 189
Nehru Rajan 11
Nelson Gallery 116
Neolithic 33, 67, *70*
Nestorians 133
nimbus 25, *114, 118-9, 197;* cf. halo
Nineveh *38*
Ning, Prince 143
Nō 135
nobles *111, 123, 126,* 134, *178-9*
nymphs 47

Old Persian 26
opera 135, 181
orange 54
ox *87-8, 126, 144;* -cart *17*

pagoda *3,* 80, *113, 123, 176-7, 178-9, 195, 205*
painters 33, 56, *73,* 80, 171, 188; cf. *under individual painters*
painting: on bricks 63f.; at court 30; development of 30f.; elements of 40, 47, *48,* 61; monochrome 36, 46, *183;* narrative 137, *155;* on pavilion 30; on robe 19; schools of 135; on standard 16; subject-matter of 83; techniques of 25, 200; cf. genre, lacquer, perspective, silk, Six Principles, tomb *and under dynasties*
palace *38,* 56, 83f., 105, *114,* 140, *155, 198, 206*
Pamirs 15, 133
Panikkar, Sardar K. 11
paper 22, 53f.
paradise garden *98;* scene 65, *84, 114,* 147, *167, 172, 173, 176-7, 178-9, 206*
parasol *120-1, 151, 205*
Paris 19, 133
partridge *58-9,* 66
Patriarchs 191

patronage 105
pavilion 106, *117*, *118-9*, *128-9*, 140, *155*
pearls 16, 134, 140
peasants 30, 185; revolt of 75
Peking 12, 47, 185
Pelliot, P. 23, 26
perspective 10, 35, 62, 64, 66, *82*, 90f., *98*, 103f., *118-9*, 140, *155*, *167*, *171*, 202, 211
Petrarch 26, 71
pheasant 66
phoenix *87-8*; tree 127
p'iao-maio *169*, *186*
pi chi 89
p'ien-wên 10
Piero della Francesca 11, *81*
pilgrims 147, *155*, *190*, *195*, 205
p'i-ma ts'un 200
pine-tree 105, *124*, 127, *137*, *164*
P'ing-Ch'êng 78
p'ing-yüan *103*, *171*
plants 54, 77; cf. ferns
play 181
plum-tree 127
Po Chü-i 134f.
poets 19f., 30, 33, 36, 53, 62, 67, 70, 80, 135, 140, *141*; poetry 61, 185; epic 80, 181; love 54, 80, 134; religious 80, 135
po-hua 107, *108*, 153
pond 30, *98*, *114*, *124*; cf. lake, lotus
poplar 22f., 26, *98*
poppy 188
portraiture *126*, 147, *151*
pottery 22, 25, 42, 54
Prabūtaratna *124*
pramāna 35
Prasenajit *94-5*
pratyaksha 35
pre-Han art 33-52, *183*; box *101*; bronzes 31; excavations 56; lacquer 45, *130*; mirror 45, 47, *48*, 130; mythology 202; painting 56; tile *130*
priest 19

prince, princess 30, 40, 147
printing 135
prison *171*
Psalter: cf. Canterbury, Utrecht
punishments 22

rabbit *58-9*, 66
Rama 36
Rāmāyana 36
rebellions 75, 134, 140, 181
reforms 185
reliefs 31, *42-3*, 43, *44-5*, 46, 50, 56, *57*, 65, 77, *87-8*, 90, *93*, *101*, *104*, 107, *108*, 116, *131*, 140, *178-9*, *193*, 203
religion 26, *178-9*, 202; cf. Buddhism, poetry, Taoism
Renaissance 10, 35, 187, 211
rice 185
rites: cf. ceremonies
river 34, 40, *40*, 42, 70, 90, *118-9*, *128-9*, 133, 140, 143, *145*, *155*, *181*, 188
rocks 30, 90, *101*, *108*, *128-9*, 168, *176-7*, 200
Roman Empire 15f., 20, 54; Rome 133
Romanesque art 10
roof 106, *108*, *110*, *128-9*, 205
rook 133
rubbings *41*, 42, *42*, *43*, *44-5*, *65*, *66*, *68*, *69*, *98*, *104*, *109*, 140, *160*, *208*
Ruru Jātaka 77
Russians 22

sacrifice 41, 66, *85*, *178-9*
Saddharma Pundarīka Sūtra *195*, 205
sages 40, *98*, 140
saints 84, *98*
Śakyamuni *93*, *124*
salt industry 53; well 55, 61, 63f.
Samarkand 15
sandalwood *151*
sandhills *183*, *193*
Śankara 191
Śankha, King *178-9*

Sanskrit   195, 205
san-tieh-fa   104
sarcophagus   109, 116, 131
Sassanians   31, 77
scarf   124
scholar   93, 211; gentry 53; poet 56
school   53, 185
Science and Civilization in China (Needham)   12
screen   178-9, 197, 198, 206, 207
scroll 44, 50, 73, 74, 84, 89, 123, 140, 141, 183,
    184
sculptor 78; sculpture 16, 30, 78, 210; cf.
    reliefs, statue
Scythians   44
shaman   42
Shang bronzes   42, 45
Shang dynasty 42; cf. pre-Han
Shang-Yin   33
shan-shui   40, 83
Shansi province   22, 195, 205
Shantung province   65, 66, 93
shell   46
shêng-tung   47
Shên Hsiu-ch'ang   53
Shensi province   43, 67, 77
shen-yüan   103
Shih Ming   40
shih-nü jên-wu   200
shih-shih jên-wu   200
shrine   118-9
Shu   143
Shun, Emperor   40
Shuo Wên   40
Sian: cf. Ch'ang-an
Sian Museum   42, 43, 67
Siddhārtha, Prince   157, 198, 206
Siena   210
silk 15, 40, 42, 178-9; books on 54; clothing 16,
    134; documents on 22, 54; painting on 53,
    56, 147, 210; scrolls 123, 147
Silk Road   15, 19
silver inlay   43, 102

silverware   31
singers   178-9
Sinkiang: cf. Sui-chien
Sirén, O.   12, 33, 140
Six Dynasties   75-104; art of 80
Six Principles of Painting   35, 83
slavery   30
soldiers   22, 30
Soper, A. C.   44, 116, 211
spices   16
spirits   40, 86, 87-8, 139, 162-3
spoon   22
spring   36, 50, 155, 192
Ssŭ T'iao   70
standard   16, 183
statue   40, 151, 161, 197
Stein, Sir A.   22ff., 26
stencil   25
stone: engraving 64; medallion 143; panel 65,
    66, 68-9; relief 65, 77, 87-8, 90, 93, 98, 104,
    107, 116, 131, 140; sarcophagus 109
stream 140, 143, 166, 171, 177, 201; cf. river
students   133, 185, 203
stūpa   18, 24, 82, 93, 143, 176-7, 205
stylization   44, 82, 183
Suddhanta Jātaka   82
Sui: art 107f., 116; affinities with Tun-huang
    210; caves 30, 190; clothing 126; dynasty
    105-132; emperors 75, 133; painting 25, 48,
    98, 106, 131, 147, 153, 155, 210; wars 19;
    Late Sui 124, 149, 168
Sui-chien   195, 205
Sukhāvatī   29
su-kuo   83
Su-lo Ho   23
sun: instrument for measuring 53; -bird 131;
    sunrise 171; sunset 89, 133, 167, 168, 169, 192
Sung: calligraphy 46; caves 200; dynasty 181-
    201, 195, 205; emperor 83; history 181, 185;
    painters 80, 187f.; painting 3, 144-5, 153,
    164, 187; poets 30, 36, 62, 80; poetry 135,
    167, 187; Early Sung 190, 197, 201

sūtra: cf. Fa-hua, Lotus, Saddharma

Su Tung-p'o 67, 91, 135, 181

swallow 77, 134

Swedes 22

symbolism 40, 42, 45, 98, 189f.

Syria 19, 54, 61

Szechwan 22, 65, 69

table 178-9

tablet 3, 151, 158, 162-4, 176-7, 178-9, 183, 197, 205, 206

Tagore, R. 35

ta-hun tien 201

T'ai Shan 41; god of 195, 205

T'ang: architecture 3; caves 30, 144-5, 147, 152, 210; dynasty 41, 66, 133-180; history 133; Lohans 151; painting 25, 48, 50, 61, 63, 65, 80, 98, 114, 132, 134, 143f., 147, 149, 152, 164, 168, 210; poets 36, 80, 135, 140, 141; reliefs 46; Early T'ang 124, 149; Late T'ang 84, 178-9, 187, 190, 197, 201; cf. Chang Yen-yüan, Hsüan-tsung

Tao 36, 67, 211f.; Taoist 34, 36, 133, 188, 200; Taoism 39, 41, 53, 61, 80, 83, 191; neo-Taoism 80

tao-shih 83, 200

T'ao Yüan-ming 80

Tarim basin 15, 23

Tarsus 134

Tartars 29

Ta-Wan: cf. Ferghana

taxation 80

tea 134

Te Hang-chia 29

temples 40, 56, 78, 84, 123, 128-9, 133, 147, 151, 205, 206, 210

tent 178-9

textiles 16, 54, 178-9

Thapar, R. 9

Three Kingdoms 75-104

ti: cf. earth

Tibet 31; Tibetan, Tibetans 24, 26, 29, 75, 155

tien 116, 120-1, 127, 168, 175, 178-9, 195, 205

t'ien: cf. heaven

T'ien Shan 15, 23

T'ien-shui 210

tien t'ai 168

tiger 16, 43, 82, 85, 93, 139

tile 49, 54, 58-9, 64, 130

Tokharian, Tokharians 26, 134

tomb: panel 52, 66, 68; painting 56, 58-9, 62, 66; relief 77, 178-9; tile 49; cf. Wu Liang-tz'ŭ

T'o-pa 78

tou-pan ts'un 200

towns 30, 137, 155, 178-9

travel, travellers 19, 22, 164, 187; cf. Hsüan Tsang, Marco Polo

Tree of Heaven 127

trees 26, 30f., 36, 40, 40, 43, 45, 44-5, 47, 48, 61f., 64, 67, 70, 82, 83, 90, 98, 107, 108, 110-1, 114, 116, 123, 130-1, 137, 149, 155, 157, 161, 173, 178-9, 192, 195, 200f., 205; cf. Bodhi, han-lin, wu-t'ung and individual species

triangle motif 42

tripod 102

ts'a jan 168

Ts'ao Yen 29

tsê 212

Tsê-liu ching 55, 61, 63

ts'un 168, 200

ts'un-fa 200

Tsung Ping 70f.

Tu Fu 134f., 181

Tung-hsuan-ssu 151

Tung-p'o: cf. Su Tung-p'o

Tun-huang: affinities with Sui art 210; description of 23f.; history of 24, 78; influence exerted by 202; influence exerted upon 31, 202; monastery at 78, 195, 205, 210; oasis of 18; painters at 171; region of 30; sculpture at 210; silk scrolls from 123; town of 9, 15, 19f., 24, 26; cf. individual caves below:

Cave 45 158, 162-4

Cave 55 198, 206, 207

Cave 61   195, 197, 205
Cave 103   137, 142
Cave 112   174, 176-7
Cave 172   171
Cave 186   186
Cave 196   178-9
Cave 198   175
Cave 205   166, 169
Cave 209   149, 152
Cave 217   66, 155, 157, 161
Cave 249   11, 87-8
Cave 257   11, 77, 79, 81, 203f.
Cave 285 10f., 43, 73, 84, 89, 96, 98, 99,
     203f.
Cave 288   190
Cave 296   11, 108, 110, 111
Cave 299   11, 101, 120-1
Cave 301   113
Cave 302   11, 112, 117, 118-9
Cave 303   126
Cave 309   29
Cave 320   167
Cave 321   139, 183
Cave 323   3, 144, 145, 151
Cave 332   193
Cave 369   173
Cave 419   114, 123, 124
Cave 420   114, 123
Cave 423   128-9
Cave 428   82, 85, 93, 96
Tung Yüan   91
Turco-Mongols   75, 78
Turfan   15
Turks   133

Uighur, Uighurs   26, 134
universities   53, 195, 205
Upanishad   191
urn   41
utensil   41
Utrecht Psalter   89

Vaidehī, Queen   171
valley   18, 24, 31
vase   60
Vedantist   191
vegetables   83
vessels   47, 48, 50, 57, 63, 70, 106, 130, 171
villages   195, 206
Vimalakīrti   114, 140
vineyard   16
Vishnu   206
Viśvantara, Prince 96; Jātaka 96

Waley, A. 10, 12, 33, 39, 65, 67, 96, 107, 137,
     157, 170, 178-9
wall   106, 108, 114, 123, 128-9
Wang An-shih   185
Wang-ch'üan   140, 141
Wang Wei   9, 31, 35, 75, 135, 140, 143
Warner, L.   178-9
Warring States   47, 57, 63, 89, 106, 130
wars 19, 30, 78; civil 75, 181; cf. battle scene
Washington, D.C.   45
watch-tower   22, 66, 155
water 40, 40, 42, 47, 55, 188f., 192, 201; water-
     clock 53; waterfall 30, 128-9, 137, 176, 201
Watts, A.W. 187
Wei: Northern 78; art 45, 77; architectural
     elements 140; caves 30; drawings 149;
     emperors 210; painting 25, 48, 83, 98, 106,
     113, 114, 147; reliefs 46, 107, 203; Late Wei
     82, 93
Wei-mo-ch'i   140
well   66, 118-9
West, the 19, 31, 151, 202f.; cf. Europe, Middle
     East
willow 98, 105, 113, 117, 118-9, 120-1, 127,
     160, 161
wind   47, 105, 181
window   106 117,
wolf   123
wood, wooden 55; boat 190; designs in 212;
     documents on 22; enclosure 206; house 117;

hut *118-9*; motif of *40*; pagoda *3*; rack 66; shrine *118-9*; strips of 54

writing-slips 22
Wu, Emperor 78
Wu, dowager Empress 80
Wu Chan 24
wu-hsing 55
Wu Liang-tz'ŭ 65, *65, 66, 68*
Wu-t'ai Shan 40, 168, *195*, 210
Wu Tao-tzŭ 30f., 67, 107, 135, 143, 168
Wu Ti, Emperor 19, *151*
Wu-Ting 20
wu-t'ung 127, *131*

yang 39, 54, *87-8*
Yang Kuei-fei 134, *164*

Yang-ti, Emperor 105f.
Yangtze-kiang 19, 105f.
Yarkand 15
Yellow River (Hwang-ho) 78, 185
Yellow Sea 133
Yen Li-pên *101*, 107
yin 39, 54, *87-8*
Yüan 135
Yüan Chi 80
Yü-Mên: cf. Jade Gate
Yün-kang cave-temples 78, 210
Yu t'ien 29

Zoroastrians 133
Zen Buddhism: cf. Ch'an